RIDING HIGH

RIDING HIGH

Ian Millar's
World of Show Jumping

IAN MILLAR AND LARRY SCANLAN

To Greg

Another riding Best!

Best Regards

"Big Ben"   *Ian D Millar*

M&S

for Lynn, my best friend, my partner, my wife

⌐

for Leonard Flynn (1892–1982) and
Gertrude Flynn (1891–1985)

CANADIAN CATALOGUING IN PUBLICATION DATA
Miller, Ian, 1947–
   Riding high
ISBN 0-7710-5872-1
1. Millar, Ian, 1947-   . 2. Show jumping.
3. Show jumpers (Horses). 4. Big Ben (Horse).
5. Show jumpers (Persons)–Canada–Biography.
I. Scanlan, Larry. II. Title.
SF295.5.M55 1990   798.2′5′092   C90-094353-X

Design: Tania Craan
Photo research: Jayne Huddleston/Equesport Canada

Printed and bound in Hong Kong

McClelland & Stewart Inc.
The Canadian Publishers
481 University Avenue
Toronto, Ontario
M5G 2E9

CONTENTS

Years ago I started a file, the first hesitant step towards a book about my life and the world of show jumping as I saw it. But the project was scuttled by lingering doubts: did I know enough about what I do? Had I accomplished enough? I am not sure I am ready now. Readers may judge for themselves.

Two things enabled this book to exist. First, Douglas Gibson, its publisher, believed from the outset in the concept of the book and that now was indeed the time for such a book. Second, I found the right ghost writer. Larry Scanlan had written a piece about me several years ago in *The Whig-Standard Magazine* in Kingston, Ontario. I had tremendous confidence in his ability as a writer and in our ability to work together.

In a sense, this book is my tribute to the horse. My first riding instructor, an entirely eccentric woman in Edmonton named Rita Gardiner, taught me as a boy that the horse was a monarch among animals. She believed it was a privilege to be associated with such a noble creature. I do love horses, and I do love show jumping, which someone once described as a game of chess played on horseback at unconscionable speed. Our country was built on the backs of horses, and even though they are now used almost exclusively for sport and leisure, I see no reason why the love and respect that our ancestors felt for horses should not endure.

The vast majority of horses are gentle, generous animals. I disagree with those who say that the dog is man's best friend. I say the horse is. My personal obsession with horses dates from the time I was five years old, sitting astride a piano bench: my first horse was a creature of my imagination.

From those first stirrings of interest in horses to the dreams that possess me now, this book covers a wide territory. In it I look back on more than twenty years of competing at the grand prix, or elite, level all over North America and Europe. Individual chapters comprise my diary of three major show-jumping tournaments in which I competed in 1989: Stuttgart in West Germany, Spruce Meadows in Calgary, and the Royal Winter Fair in Toronto. Big Ben, my million-dollar mount who continues to astound me with his achievements, and who may, with luck, retire some years from now with a winning record unmatched in the sport, looms large throughout this chronicle. So do the many other horses I have ridden, some of them wonderful, some of them — in my more distant past — as headstrong and green as their young rider.

I hope that in these pages even experienced horsewomen and horsemen will make discoveries — about the training of horses or the teaching of riders, for example — and that readers new to show jumping will be able to make more sense of it all. The book is neither purely instructive nor purely personal; I hope it is a bit of both. It is the story of a man who rides and trains horses at the world-class level. It poses the question, "What does it take to be a champion at that level?" and ponders the answer.

How does one ride and train a grand prix horse? How does one manage to stay aboard grand prix horses when the cost of such mounts reaches unimaginable heights? What is a "day in the life" like on the road, or at home? How did I find Big Ben, and what makes him special? These questions and many others I have attempted to answer.

But mine is not the only voice heard in this book. The thoughts of fifteen prominent personalities in the sport — interviewed by Larry Scanlan at competitions in Canada and Europe in 1989 — have been collected and strategically placed throughout the book.

I do not see my life in dramatic terms, but others might. Certainly, my discovery of Big Ben was a turning point, and there have been some bleak moments when circumstances — crippling debt in the early years, and later a painful and recurring back injury that put my career on ice — seemed tilted against any real chance of success. But I have always been an optimist, even through the worst of times. From the beginning, there was never any question, in my mind anyway, that a life with horses was in the cards for me.

In my youth, crossing the country in a railway boxcar with a horse named Bonnie Dundee, I could not have imagined that one day I would be honoured with the Order of Canada, acquire the nickname "Captain Canada", or that I would experience the exhilaration of back-to-back World Cup victories. But neither could I have imagined a life without horses.

This is the story of that life, told honestly and candidly, and the story of the many people who helped make possible whatever success I have enjoyed. No one deserves more thanks than my family. My wife Lynn, son Jonathon, daughter Amy, and, especially in the beginning, my parents, Doris and Livingstone Millar, have shared in my passion and, better still, understood it.

Ian D. Millar,
Perth, Ontario
March 1990

RIDING HIGH

CHAPTER I

Stuttgart: A Diary

*M*onday, *October 23, 1989*: I used to like travel, but the road does not beckon the way it once did. The problem is not the tournaments: I *love* being at competitions. I only wish they were all in Perth, down the road from our own Millar Brooke Farm in southeastern Ontario. In the past twenty years I have been to more than six hundred horse shows all over North America and Europe. Getting ready to leave for West Germany, I am reminded — as I always am when I hit the road one more time — of how much there is to be done at home and how little time.

Paula Heinemann, my Australian-born assistant and still occasional nanny to our children, creates long lists of things I must do before my wife, Lynn, and I drive to Mirabel Airport to catch our flight to Frankfurt and Stuttgart. By 3:00 P.M. Monday most items are checked off. Even so, we seek out a telephone kiosk at Mirabel — one of those circular ones —

Wotan jumps a wide water jump.
(Howard Rosenberg)

I

to say our last-minute goodbyes to son Jonathon and daughter Amy and to talk to the business associates we could not reach earlier that day. With Lynn on one phone and me on the one beside it, we sometimes do a quick switch, which must amuse onlookers, when we both need to converse with the same two people.

Big Ben, my top horse, and the eight-year-old mare Lonesome Dove were sent off Saturday morning in a Boeing 747 Combi with their groom, Sandi Patterson. Like human travellers, horses crossing international borders must have passports. The passport lists the horse's veterinary background, blood tests, and vaccinations, and serves as identification. Horse passports were meant to facilitate border crossings, but they remain a tangled business.

At Mirabel there is no crowd, so the Lufthansa people have time to chat. "Why Stuttgart?" they ask. "Horse show," I explain, and make the connection to the horses sent off from Mirabel on Saturday. "Beautiful horses," one remembers, and wishes us luck.

Stuttgart is one of the most important indoor tournaments in the world, and we are hoping to do well. This is my third trip to a show that has been reasonably good to us: one of our horses, Future Shock, won a major class (individual event) there once, and Big Ben was second in the grand prix competition. Usually held at the end of better horse shows, the grand prix, as its name implies, is an event with a lucrative prize. Generally, any rider over eighteen years of age is technically eligible to compete, but the high and demanding fences ensure that only elite horses and riders do.

Stuttgart marks Big Ben's first indoor show in almost a year, and he usually takes a show or two to make the transition, especially after a light summer. Outdoor shows seem more natural to horses; indoor shows tax them both physically and mentally. Our goal is to peak Big Ben for the Royal Winter Fair next month in Toronto and then again for the World Cup next April in Dortmund, West Germany. What a delicate art that is! When a horse peaks, you can only hold him there for a short time. There are just so many wins in a great horse, and once he hits his prime, you begin to count down. You are spending, like a pitcher in major-league baseball who has only so many victories left. What we want to do with Big Ben is maximize that spending power.

As for Lonesome Dove, she is a promising young German-bred mare (an Oldenburg) with one grand prix win — at the Tournament of Champions in Newmarket, Ontario, a month ago — to her credit. I renamed her after watching a TV mini-series based on a novel by the American writer Larry McMurtry about a Wild West town called Lonesome Dove. I liked the name, I very much liked the TV series, and I love this horse. If you have a good mare, you have the best horse of all. She can do the impossible for you, and a good one will never give up, whereas a gelding

On Lonesome Dove.
Mares can be cantanker-
ous and moody, but if you
have a good mare, you
have the best horse of all.
(Anita Antonucci/*Ottawa
Sun*)

(a castrated stallion) might. But mares can be cantankerous and moody, and this is why there are so few of them in show jumping. Lonesome Dove is no exception: three months ago I was unable even to get her to turn. She has also been nervous and head-shy — sudden movements in her visual range can spook her. We are entering her in only two classes here; such limited competition reduces the odds of winning.

I like to fly business class. The extra-wide seats and leg room are better suited to my six-foot-two frame. I remove my shoes, take what sleep I can, drink lots of soda water. I try to fend off jet lag, but the enemy is relentless. Close friends marvel at my stamina, but it does have limits.

Bleary-eyed stopover in Frankfurt. Change some Canadian dollars into Deutschmarks. The coffee in the Frankfurt airport restaurant is overpriced and very strong. I begin to think about my life, which sometimes seems rich and diverse — I meet corporate lions and high-ranking politicians, powerful and often interesting people — and at other times dreadfully narrow: horses, just horses. I begin conversing with someone beside me in the restaurant about books I have not read and likely never will, the world of the deaf and sign language, things I know nothing about. What contribution, I sometimes wonder, am I making to the scheme of things? But these doubts trouble me only occasionally. I ride and train horses. This is what I do, and, as Lynn would say, between the jigs and the reels I do it well. Curiously, I have no idols or heroes. I admire qualities in certain people or envy a certain skill they possess, but I never think I would like to trade places with anyone.

Tuesday, October 24: We touch down at Stuttgart in the southeastern part of West Germany. At the bottom of the stairs as we descend from the plane is Hauke Schmidt, the course designer for the Stuttgart tournament. Handshakes for me, flowers for Lynn. Mercedes-Benz is one of the sponsors of the show, and one of their cars is waiting for us on the runway. Once we have our luggage we are whisked to the stables near Hanns-Martin-Schleyer-Halle where the competition will take place. Named after a Mercedes-Benz executive who was murdered by terrorists about eight years ago, the *Halle* has been transformed into an elegant show ring, with Dutch flowers adorning the corners. In many ways, it's a typical indoor ring — the size of a hockey rink, with boards, but soft footing instead of ice. The *Halle* is also a velodrome. Partially hidden behind bleachers, wooden parquet floors — banked at a thirty-three-degree angle in the corners for the cyclists' sake — rise up some thirty feet from ground level. But that design also cuts into seating space, so capacity is a modest 7,500.

There is a long tradition here both of show jumping and of dressage — a form of precise riding often likened to ballet, in which riders, dressed very formally in tails and top hats, ask their horses to execute dance-like manoeuvres. Both equestrian sports are very much admired and appreciated in Europe, more so than in North America. Stuttgart is one of the wealthiest cities in West Germany, and every competition will be sold out. Scalpers make a killing on the street. A week's pass to the show is 300 Deutschmarks, or some $200 Canadian. The reigning European Champion, the great British rider John Whitaker on Milton, is the darling of the crowd. The only Canadian rider here, I am clearly also favoured to win.

When I get to the stall under the huge circus tents where Big Ben, Lonesome Dove, and the other horses are kept, half a dozen reporters

*With course designer
Hauke Schmidt*
(Hans Donner)

and photographers are waiting for me. By the weekend there will be 180 journalists here. I wish I spoke some German. Many here do speak English, some perfectly. Others put an interesting twist on pronunciation. One calls me *Eye*-on. *Eye*-on Mill-*are*. After a quick scrum with the reporters and some posed shots with Big Ben (whose profile is even higher in Europe than in Canada), I get to work. The horses, I learn from Sandi, had a trouble-free trip — until Frankfurt. There, separated briefly from his pal Lonesome Dove, Big Ben had become anxious and flung one leg over the wooden stall (an open box about five feet high) in which he was travelling. He managed to get the leg back by himself, but there was a sizeable bruise on his chest as a souvenir.

Normally Big Ben travels well enough. We give him what Lynn calls his ''magic drops'' before shipping him anywhere. This is a herbal concoction available only in West Germany, and we put twenty drops of the stuff in his feed before he sets out. Canadian vets assure us that the herbs do no harm, but doubt they do much good. Lynn swears by them. I am not at all superstitious, nor do I believe in magic, but clearly these magic drops seem to work. An added bonus of coming to West Germany is that we can pick up another batch.

Moving horses by plane requires care and planning. The horses are first loaded into the ''crates'', or portable stalls, at the airport, and a ''high-loader'' machine then hydraulically lifts each stall into the air until it is level with the cargo door of the plane. The stalls are covered, so the horse is not aware of being thrust into the air. When the stall is level with the aircraft, rollers are activated to move it into the plane, where brackets hold it in place.

Horses are loaded into special air-cargo "crates", in the same way they would enter a horse trailer. The crate is then loaded onto the aircraft.
(Jayne Huddleston)

The horses are also fitted with neck straps. These are meant to prevent horses from lifting their heads and banging them in a moment of panic, and also to prevent horses from getting out of their stalls. I would not want to be on a plane transporting horses without neck straps. If a horse ever got loose and kicked a hole in the plane, the entire aircraft would be imperilled. KLM, the Dutch airline, is most experienced in international horse transport, and puts a specially trained horse attendant on board. That person monitors the horses throughout the flight and carries in his equipment bag a drug to kill a horse should that be necessary.

Coming back from the Munich Olympics in 1972, both riders and horses of the Canadian equestrian team were on the same DC-8 when one horse (who was not wearing a neck strap) did go crazy. He got one leg outside the stall, and we would have had to destroy him had he got loose. But we managed to get the leg back in, and then he decided to lie on the bottom of his pallet. Halfway across the ocean he got back up and he was fine after that.

Sometimes the change in air pressure on take-off and landing bothers the horses' ears, and then they are given carrots to munch, much as humans chew gum to alleviate the discomfort from pressure. Horses seem to have one advantage in flying: as far as I can tell, they suffer no significant jet lag.

In the training ring, it is obvious that Big Ben and Lonesome Dove have not been exercised in three days. Until today the facilities had been tied up with international gymnastic and tennis competitions, leaving nowhere for Sandi even to walk the horses. The result is extreme friskiness and playfulness on Big Ben's part. Lonesome Dove, especially, is all rested up and ready to assert herself.

6

One side of my mouth is crusted and cut, my lower lip blistered, the result of a fall in the ring at Millar Brooke Farm a few days back. A young horse had gotten tangled up in a jump and my face had been driven deep into the ground. On average I fall off a horse — or with a falling horse — five or six times a year. Mine is a dangerous sport, and I should wear a helmet during training, as all riders should. I do try to remember, and more and more now I do remember. Old dog, new trick.

By now it is mid-afternoon. We have just enough time to get back to the hotel for a shower before dinner at the home of Hauke Schmidt and his wife, Marie. Dinner is an elegant, six-course affair, catered by six impeccably mannered youths from the Lufthansa catering service. We drink champagne and fine wines from this area of Germany (called Swabia), the bottles sleeved in white linen, and eat lamb filet that comes with a Swabian noodle specialty called *Schupfnudeln*, caviar... It seems there is rarely a middle ground in show jumping. You can win for a long stretch, and then go through a dry patch. You either jump on ground as hard as concrete or on perfect footing. It is either fried chicken under a tent at the Collingwood Horse Show in Ontario, or this memorable meal in a grand country home near Stuttgart.

Later in the evening, after more Swabian wine, cross-table talk grows more lively. My friend Hans Pracht, a horseman and still an active dressage rider at the age of sixty-four, who left Germany for Canada eight years ago, confidently predicts that I will win the Mercedes-Benz car offered as a prize in a class at the Stuttgart show. Just as confidently, Claus Kramer, the German-born owner of several horses on the Swiss national team, throws down a thousand-Deutschmark note on the table. Claus is very thin, slightly crippled on one side, and his voice never rises above a hoarse whisper — the results of a horrible helicopter accident some years before. Claus bets that I will win neither the car *nor* the grand prix; Hans puts a Canadian hundred-dollar bill on the table that says I will win one or both. Bets are on; Marie Schmidt agrees to act as the bank.

Wednesday, October 25: Dressage riders occupy the training ring most of the morning, offering me a rare chance to sleep in a bit. The days are unusually warm and sunny; sweaters and coats stay in the hotel closet.

The view from the fifth floor of the Hotel Europe is of a modern city set in a valley. Below, they are building what looks like a concrete flying saucer, huge cranes are everywhere, but up on a hillside overlooking the city are vast vineyards. Grapes growing on prime commercial land: this has always amazed me about Stuttgart. I am told that the conditions are perfect on that hillside for grapes, which are cultivated in neat Teutonic rows.

Much separates European and North American show-jumping competitions. Well-organized and sponsored, drawing the best riders, the one in Stuttgart is quite formal, a polished production that runs on time. Spruce Meadows in Calgary is at least its equal, but the Royal Winter Fair in Toronto is the only other Canadian show that might compare. While dressage and show jumping are paired in European tournaments, that rarely happens in North America, where the two disciplines attract different audiences. In Canada and the United States, hunters and show jumpers almost always compete at the same site; in Europe, save for Britain, hunters don't exist at all.

Another difference is that the stabling area in Stuttgart is off-limits to spectators; unlimited access to stables in Canada is increasingly becoming a problem as the sport draws greater interest. And the financing is not the same at all: in North America, riders' entry fees are high, there are many exhibitors (such as saddle-makers and others) who also pay high fees for their space, and corporate sponsorship is hard to come by. In Europe, entry fees for riders are low, there are few exhibitors, tickets to the show are expensive, and corporate and media interest is greater. Ironically, it cost Millar Brooke Farm a great deal more to show in Calgary or Halifax, Canada, in 1989 than in Stuttgart, West Germany.

Someone once called show jumping in North America a private-enterprise sport. The Canadian circuit has the appearance of cohesiveness, with some eighteen to twenty major shows across Canada. The Canadian Equestrian Federation provides a set of rules by which show-jumping competitions are run and has some control over the timing of official competitions. Beyond that each show is independent. But for the fact that the Canadian Equestrian Federation has jurisdiction over the rules (in fact, it owns the rules and dictates when they might be used), shows in different provinces could in theory conflict, and a big show could wipe out a smaller one by drawing away the best horses and riders.

Some people make a living managing and organizing horse shows in North America. New shows pop up and die every year. Canadian riders tend to ride their own circuit, as well as others — in the northeastern United States, Florida, Arizona, and, in some cases, Europe. The costs for riders on the circuit in entry and stall fees alone are staggering. In 1989, that figure for me approached $200,000; travel, hotel, staff, and other expenses came close to doubling the bill.

The consensus among riders is that the European circuit is far more professionally run and co-ordinated, in the way that sports such as big-league baseball and football are organized in North America. Greater interest by spectators, corporations, and the media ensure that the quality of shows on the European circuit rarely dips below a certain standard. My hope is that North American show jumping will move in the direction of the European model.

The fans in Stuttgart are knowledgeable and the sport is extraordinarily popular. Owing to the long history of equestrian sports in Europe, journalists here know more and ask tougher questions. But it also means that riders become public figures. When a prominent German horseman dismissed a rider in his stable because the rider and the horseman's wife were having an affair, the European media feasted on the whole messy business. I have trouble with that. I agree to interviews and sign autographs because I perceive it as my responsibility to the sport. But at heart I am more a private person.

European fans know a lot about riders' lives. But they also know the subtleties and the etiquette of competitive riding. If horse and rider are still clear approaching the last fence, sometimes a buzz will run through the crowd. But as the buzz rises, others in the crowd shush for silence. I am a purist, and I admire other purists. These fans want no noise to disturb the horse's or the rider's focus. When the course is completed, that is when the applause erupts.

Another difference is that in Europe there are few women riders at the top, which is lamentable. Perhaps they cannot handle the traditionally rugged and heavy horses used here, although female riders in North America seem capable of it. In Europe, women are not allowed to wear the red jackets that male national team members wear, which puzzles me. Perhaps that all may change. German breeders are going to a lighter, more sensitive horse by introducing more blood lines from the American thoroughbred. One day female riders in Europe may reach the top *and* wear the red jackets.

Stuttgart is a first-rate show but not without its problems. The stables area cross a busy four-lane thoroughfare from the *Halle*. Flagmen have to stop traffic to let horses and riders cross. This is definitely a show

Paul Schockemöhle
(Jayne Huddleston)

for senior horses; younger, more excitable horses could not cope. And since Europeans like to combine dressage and show jumping at a single competition – dressage events during the day, show jumping in the evening – that means limited training time for riders.

For Lynn and me, the Stuttgart show is a departure from most others, and in some ways, more relaxing. We often have between eight and twelve horses at a show; here we have only two, meaning less work, more spare time. I am seeing new horses and I am always on the lookout for one to buy.

A prominent horseman named Paul Schockemöhle is here. When he rode for West Germany, he was a shrewd strategist. A good rider, certainly, but just as important, he was smart: he rode horses that suited him. He found a now-legendary horse named Deister and built a career around that horse, going on to become a three-time European Champion during the 1980s. Paul also became a brilliant businessman.

The Germans are the biggest breeders of sport horses in the world, and Paul Schockemöhle is a major player. His operation in northern Germany is incredible. There are 230 stalls and 60 grooms on his farm, and the auction he conducts the first week of December – called Performance Sales International – is the biggest of its kind in the world. In 1988, the sale took in 8.48 million Deutschmarks ($5.6 million Canadian), and the average horse sold for 143,000 Deutschmarks ($94,000 Canadian). Paul picks the jumpers for the sale, and a horseman named Ulli Kasselmann selects the dressage horses. Both are highly respected. I look at the glossy hardbound catalogue they have published

to plug the sale and mention to "Schock" that there might be a few horses I would be interested in, but I do not pursue the matter. In horse-dealing, it is best not to appear too eager.

Paul Schockemöhle, veteran German grand prix rider and three-time European Champion during the 1980s

Great riders have to have talent, and Ian, for sure, has it. I saw him for the first time in 1973 when I rode the fall circuit — Washington, New York, and Toronto — but it was unbelievable how much he improved later on. He wasn't a bad rider then, but he became a superstar. He made himself by his will and by his brain. He is very clever.

He would never do a stupid thing in the ring. Everything he does, you see the brain behind it. He is a super horseman in all senses of the word. Taking care of horses, riding and training different horses, getting the maximum out of them in the ring every time, keeping them going for a long time: that's all horsemanship and the difference between a top jockey and a merely good jockey.

His mind is always under control. Ian has courage, and that's a part of riding, but not a big part. Some people have too much courage and they don't control themselves. He always makes up his mind before he goes into the ring what to do.

He takes his job very seriously. What he did in the last World Cup was absolutely brilliant. He won all three competitions, and look at how he won. After his horse didn't jump the best at the Olympic Games, to come back, to prepare the horse for the World Cup, that was really great. I never saw him as hungry. Every good competitor has to be cool. John Whitaker, Michael Matz, these riders ride the same under pressure, even better. I always rode better under pressure than in just the normal class, because I concentrated more.

Ian's riding style is what we say in German homogen. *It means "homogenized", and in riding it means going with the horse, fluidly with the movement of the horse, never against the horse. He doesn't disturb the horse; he's got a quiet style. It's important that show-jumping riders not disturb horses too much with hands or legs. It takes the horse's concentration away from the jumps.*

Ian will only get better. I see him competing at least another ten years. He has no weaknesses; as a European I would like to see some weaknesses in him. But there are none.

After buying European horses for many years, I have noticed that countries tend to breed a show jumper in character not unlike their own. The German horse, for example, tends to be exceptionally talented, a little on the cold side in terms of his disposition, and needs a great deal of repetition and structure in his life. A joke about the Hanoverian breed (which could as easily be told about other breeds, not just German ones) goes, "Why did German soldiers ride Hanoverians to war?" Answer: "So they'd be good and mad when they got there." Once the German horse is trained, however, you have a superior horse.

Wednesday afternoon some of the riders are invited to the Mercedes-Benz test track outside the city where the cars are torture-tested. The whole area is the size of a football field, with courses marked out by plastic, cone-shaped pylons. We are invited to do a little torture-testing of our own.

After being divided into groups of four or five, we are assigned four test routines. Our times are recorded by Mercedes engineers using portable computers, so that while fun is intended here, competitive instincts are also aroused. One of the tests, for example, is to drive over a snaking course covering partially wet asphalt; another requires that you reach a speed of sixty kilometres per hour on a straightaway before braking and then veering to avoid an obstacle, again on wet pavement. Too fast on either course, and the pylons get mowed down, and you lose points. Too slow, the pylons stay up, but you lose anyway. Not so different from riding a horse in the show ring. One of the Dutch riders is an utter maniac on the course; the pylons come down like bowling pins.

My favourite is what the engineers call the "Mickey Mouse" course, I suppose because of its shape. You drive a super-modified, 320-horsepower Mercedes fitted with roll bar and wide racing tires. Touch the gas pedal and the tires screech, the engine growls. You take the course as fast as you can — your teeth grinding, your arms shaking on the wheel, your whole body tottering on that line between control and loss of control — without wiping out pylons. Two laps take just over one hundred seconds, and every rider emerges from the car smiling. The whole experience is intoxicating.

I like speed. I keep thinking how that car would perform on the *Autobahn*, the German highway where there are long stretches without speed limits.

I spend the evening on business calls. Paula lines them up from Perth because North Americans can call Europe more cheaply than the reverse. Tomorrow we will finally begin to compete.

Thursday, October 26: I like to get to a competition early, especially for grand prix events. I steep myself in the atmosphere for up to two hours beforehand.

Lonesome Dove's first stab at European competition goes well. Only one rail down in her class, but her time is fast. Fritz Bollinger, a Swiss-born engineering consultant who lives near Kingston, Ontario, is here with his wife, Lilian, for the competition; the Bollingers, along with Nell and Don Elliott and Millar Brooke Farm, are co-owners of Lonesome Dove. One of the brightest men I know, Fritz takes a keen eye to competitions, and when he talks afterwards, I listen. After the class, he reminds me that part-way through the event, a group of photographers were brought into the ring and positioned beside jump number five. Fritz further points out that few horses and riders made it over fence number five as long as the photographers were gathered there. The minute they left, the fence ceased to be a "bogey" fence, the one causing everyone trouble. Did they rattle the horses? Hard to say; but fence number five was Lonesome Dove's undoing.

Big Ben and I have even less success. Hauke Schmidt's courses are challenging, with lots of turns and open jumps with gaps below the rails that make it hard for the horses to measure distances. We have two rails down for eight penalties or faults. Faults are charged when the horse knocks down an obstacle, when horse or rider fall, or when the horse refuses to jump a fence. A plank fell first; maybe I turned Ben too soon. The end result is that we are well down the list in this qualifying event, and unless we come up big on Friday in the second qualifier, there will be no Mercedes-Benz for us.

Tonight we relax with some of the other riders in the bar of the hotel. Among riders the accent is always on winning, but when the competition is over, it is over. We do business with each other, we exchange training ideas. Ours is a sport of constant discovery. Much of what we do is visible: if a rider develops a different bit or a warm-up technique, we come to share those things. The German *chef d'équipe*, or team manager, Herbert Meyer, has an expression – "friends by night" – that nicely captures the feeling among riders. Ours is a small and tight little world.

*John Whitaker and Milton
in Stuttgart*
(Jayne Huddleston)

On a whim, I decide to give my Snowy River hat to John Whitaker. John is an outstanding horseman and an extremely efficient rider. I could pay him no higher compliment than that. He looks right at home in the hat. Sitting deep in his chair, he tips the hat up on his brow with his index finger, the way cowboys do. He may be British, but he has seen enough westerns to know what to do with an Australian outback hat.

I have long felt that the British are the best horsemen in the world. They take excellent care of their horses: rails first became lighter and cups (metal supports for the rails) shallower at British shows — after riders insisted on it. The end result is "careful jumping", and horses that compete longer and are still jumping well at seventeen and eighteen years of age. North America later caught on to the notion of careful jumping, but the British were the forerunners.

I go to bed thinking of Fritz and Lilian Bollinger. It was on this same weekend eight years ago that their son André died in a tragic accident. He was electrocuted at home while helping his brother Claude and some others put up a TV antenna. André was only twenty-six and very well liked. He was my close friend as well as my student, and he was just about to ride on the Canadian equestrian team. I gave the eulogy at his funeral, and I will never forget what a horrendous time this was. Fritz and Lilian have long been my supporters and friends, but for many years it must have been hard for them to be near me. The healing is slow from a wound like that, and never complete.

Friday, October 27: This evening is round two of the qualifying rounds to name the Jumping Master, the winner who will drive away in the new Mercedes. Big Ben and I have to come in among the top five, or there is no going on to the final round later this evening.

14

Springer, one of my earlier mounts, jumping (almost) a puissance wall.

Somehow Big Ben *knows* when he is going to compete. Thursday morning he was pawing the ground in his stall, bobbing his head, wanting to go. Tonight he has to be right on.

It does go well, for a time. Big Ben and I make one daring inside turn, a risky move that passes up a safer, wide approach to a jump in favour of a short-cut between two obstacles. The move can leave a horse ill-prepared for the sudden appearance of the subsequent jump. Our time is the best of the bunch. But one rail comes down. We are out of it. The car will go to John Whitaker on Milton.

Tomorrow. Maybe tomorrow with Lonesome Dove.

Saturday, October 28: At this competition and at many others there is a silly custom called the costume class. I duck it when I can — and I do here. In Stuttgart the silliness reaches new heights. One German rider enters the ring with his horse dressed as a cow, complete with udder and horns. A horse ridden by Joe Turi, a British rider, lies on the ground with its legs up in the air before Joe climbs on the horse's belly, as if to ride. One year the French rider Philippe Rozier "water-skied" behind his horse. But the favourite in Stuttgart is Kevin Bacon, the Australian-born legend in his late fifties who still rides the grand prix circuit. He has a four-year-old horse who follows him around a course of jumps while Kevin rides another horse. The horse will fetch his hat, lift handkerchiefs out of pockets, and come and stay on command. The crowd loves every bit of it.

Later I am sitting in the stands eating ice-cream and watching the puissance. In French, the word *puissance* means "power". In show jumping, the word describes a class to determine which horse and rider can jump the highest: the world indoor record is just several inches shy of eight feet. But it is a controversial event. You are essentially showing the horse what he *cannot* do. This is normally a class for specialty horses, brave, rugged animals who can leap mountains. There is nothing wrong with the class as long as the right horses are used. But as the competition stiffens and the wall is made ever higher, I note that a layer of big heavy blocks lies just under the lighter rounded ones at the top. Because the heavier blocks are harder to dislodge, more horses go on to compete in the final, but that also means harder knocks. This puissance is not exactly horse-friendly.

The puissance is over. Now comes our turn. How will Lonesome Dove fare in this big test? In this, the "joker" class, the first fence is worth one point, the second fence two points, and so on, until you come to the ninth and tenth fences. The tenth fence is the joker fence: jump it and you gain double its value, or twenty points; down it and you *lose* twenty points. Another option is to avoid the number-ten fence altogether, and try the fence to the left of it, the less challenging number-nine fence, worth nine points. This is not a speed class, in which the rider with the fewest faults and fastest time wins. But there is a time limit, with penalties for exceeding it. A certain number of riders will advance to the jump-off, in which speed *is* the deciding factor.

As Lonesome Dove enters the ring, Lynn is in the crowd, growing more alarmed by the second. The horse is looking at the spectators, not at the job ahead. Lynn tells me afterwards that she was thinking, almost out loud, "Look at the jumps, Dovey! Look at the jumps!" But Lonesome Dove manages the course beautifully, even vaulting the big joker fence that has beaten so many other riders. But as I look back up to the computer board while leaving the ring, I do not see 65 points beside my name. I see 64.75. I have exceeded the time allotted by less than a second. I can hardly remember the last time I had a time-fault. That quarter time-fault will keep us out of the jump-off.

Never mind. I am pleased. More pleased than most people could imagine. Lonesome Dove has jumped beautifully, and even had we competed in the jump-off, I would not have pushed her: a fifth or a sixth is the best we could have hoped for. This early in her development, I want her confidence high. Nothing wrong with our eleventh-place ribbon for such an inexperienced horse and in such a class field. Sometimes people fail to understand how I can be happy with such a placing. They think I am snatching victory from defeat, falling prey to false optimism. "Short-term goals," I tell them, "have to be consistent with long-term goals." It took me a long time to learn that lesson. The pressures to win *today* can seem immense, but I will resist them if the win comes at the expense of certain wins *tomorrow*. I like the tortoise-and-the-hare analogy: the hare is faster, but sometimes the tortoise wins in the long run. Fortunately, whenever I have longed for short-term gains, people such as Lynn or friends whose judgement I trust were there to argue against it. With maturity, you learn not to be seduced by the short term.

Later, about six other grooms make a point of telling Sandi how well they thought Lonesome Dove had jumped. There is often a nice feeling of community among grooms at these international events. Yogurt, says Sandi, has the value of currency here. She has been trading glass containers of yogurt for books, small favours, and on the last day, a European voltage extension cord. She stays at a small hotel near the stables. One morning she arrives at the stalls to find a block of Swiss chocolate on the Millar Brooke Farm trunk. A German citizen who once worked as a groom has remembered her from a previous competition in Tampa, Florida. More currency. . . .

The "old guys" on the European circuit are doing well here. David Broome of Britain, Nelson Pessoa (he rides for Brazil but has lived in Europe for decades), and Kevin Bacon have all won ribbons and cash. David is the youngster in that group; he is forty-nine, and before John Whitaker emerged, he was perhaps the most efficient rider in the sport. Nelson is fifty-three. Kevin, the oldest at fifty-seven, tells me that no amount of money could persuade him to pass up the joys of riding and competing. He drives a beat-up horse van and possesses one of the most unorthodox riding styles I have ever seen. European spectators sense his boundless and ageless enthusiasm. He won a grand prix a few weeks back. Tonight he takes a fifth in the joker competition and the audience applauds wildly when he takes off his hat in appreciation. But this is not why he rides, to please crowds. He just loves — and I mean *loves* — what he does. "It's not a sport," he says, "it's a disease." But he feels privileged to be so afflicted.

Australian Kevin Bacon, at fifty-seven one of the oldest competitors on the circuit
(Howard Rosenberg)

David Broome, veteran grand prix rider and former World Champion, Great Britain

A great rider is one who wins a lot of classes on a lot of different horses. Our sport has seen the rise and fall of many jockeys who've been superb on one horse. When the horse disappears, so do they. Ian fits the bill of the great rider, and I would have to say, against physical odds. To his credit, he looks neat on a horse, which is not easy for a man that size. Even Ian on a seventeen-hand horse looks neat. He rides in a style that makes the sport look easy — the sign of a champion.

I spoke to Ian three weeks before the World Cup in Tampa, and he was a little worried about how his horse was going. I thought his horse was jumping well, though he wasn't winning. But consider Ian's achievement: to win the first day; sleep on it that night; win the next day; then two days off. There are a lot of hours to sleep at night when perhaps you don't sleep as well as you ought to, and to actually come out the last day and still put in two more faultless performances, that must put him in a league very much on his own. There were a lot of people there with very good horses trying to knock him off his pedestal, and nobody got close. It showed that he can stand the mental pressures.

That's important. A horse will get anxious if the rider is nervous. But that's only the sport in the ring. There's a managerial part of Ian that exceeds that of most people. He can plan, he can train, and he can produce for the moment. When he was in Tampa — this was during competition before the World Cup — Ian wasn't concerned about winning every class, he was quietly taking his horse to its peak. His target was the World Cup.

Personally, I hate big horses. Here we have Big Ben, 17.3 hands. He really is a cute big devil, but there were times when he wasn't a cute big devil. He was a big clunk. And for someone to train him to be so careful and so quick, it doesn't happen very often. I couldn't imagine anybody doing a better job on Big Ben than Ian. He trained him from a 17.3-hand horse that nobody would look at into a world star. No easy job.

He rides forward. He schools his horses so he rides forward. On Big Ben he can take strides out between fences so easily. And he has a great eye and balance to do that. He can keep the hocks underneath him on a forward stride; not many people have that talent.

I had a very interesting conversation with Ian at the Olympic Games in Seoul, about some of the problems in our sport. We just sat together in the stands by pure chance. Ian thinks. His thoughts on the sport, the direction it should go: I found those as thoughtful and accurate and as good as anyone's could be. We were talking about training horses and cruelty to horses and what's going on. He was very concerned about that and had definite thoughts. He doesn't see it increasing, but he sees warning bells ringing, and he knows the consequences if it got out of hand. We're a public-image sport. I was very inspired by what he said. He's a leader. I would like to think that the future of the sport could lie very safely in his hands in the years to come if he ever took up administration.

Ian is very good with people. He always has time. We Europeans are wary of the American friendship angle — "Have a nice day." In many cases it's false. Ian is not false. He's genuine.

A narrow vertical can sometimes unsettle a horse. Big Ben jumps one at Spruce Meadows.
(Jayne Huddleston)

At one point, when the arena is not being used for competition, a sponsor is given the chance to ride John Whitaker's superb grey, Milton. I can picture the man, almost boyishly making the request to ride the great horse, and John Whitaker, just as boyishly, saying, "Sure." The fellow, in his sixties, turns out to be a fair rider, and he attempts – and pulls off, to the delight of everyone there – a flying change on Milton. In the flying change, the rider instructs the horse, on the fly, to stop leading with his left front leg and instantly switch to the right lead, or vice-versa.

Tomorrow is Sunday. The Grand Prix of Stuttgart. Looking on the bright side, we have shown that Lonesome Dove can travel and handle European competition, and Big Ben has one more indoor show under his belt. But if nothing comes of tomorrow, Hans Pracht loses his bet and we go home empty-handed. A long way to come for that. Tomorrow or nothing.

Sunday, October 29: Big Ben knows it is Grand Prix day. He is primed and ready. We draw sixth in a field of forty-one, not ideal. I would rather watch others go before me and learn from their mistakes. The course is tough, full of tight 180-degree turns. A narrow "vertical" was our undoing at Spruce Meadows in Calgary a few months back. A vertical is a single fence flanked by vertical standards, which tests the horse's ability to jump a height, as opposed to a wide or "spread" jump, which forces the horse to jump both height and width. Narrow verticals unsettle horses because the space through which they must jump may seem to them disturbingly small. Here there are two narrow verticals separated by a gallop the length of the arena. The course designer's trick is this: the horse is stretched for the gallop and then suddenly has to be collected to make the vertical.

But the course seems beatable. Three riders go clear before me. Our time is a fairly slow one, but we do go clear. As the other riders follow, it is obvious that those narrow verticals are the bogey fences. Ten riders retire before completing the course, many of them after knocking down *both* verticals. By the end of round one there have been fifteen clear rounds. On to round two. Survivors will proceed to a jump-off. I watch all this from the crowd, with Lynn, but not where riders normally sit as a group. I want no one to disrupt my focus.

Round two. Ben and I go clear again, this time in the fastest time. In fact, the format of two rounds and a jump-off is unusual for us, and Big Ben is convinced that round two is the jump-off. He wants to go faster; I have to hold him back. In the end, four others proceed to the jump-off: Kurt Maier, Jr., of West Germany on Leon, Jos Lansink of The Netherlands on Felix, Thomas Fruhmann of Austria on Grandeur, and Nick Skelton of Great Britain on Grand Slam.

Now the pressure is really on. I aim to win. Allowed 47 seconds over the shortened course, we go first. Big Ben covers a lot of ground with those long strides of his; he is deceptively fast. We go clean in a time of 32:76. Now I must look on helplessly as the others go. But going first has its advantages. If your time is fast enough, you put pressure on those after you, and if they press, they make mistakes. The others know how fast Ben is, and they do press, taking down at least one rail each. The Grand Prix of Stuttgart and 30,000 Deutschmarks (almost $20,000 Canadian) are ours.

The big computer board reads:

1. BIG BEN   I. MILLAR   CAN   32:76

It is a victory to savour. Hauke Schmidt has shown himself to be an aggressive course designer. Most North American course designers would have backed off in the second round in order to let eight or twelve riders into the jump-off. Although riders do not approve, it has become fashionable to turn the grand prix jump-off into a speed class. Not Hauke. He *raised* the skinny vertical. I admire that.

Big Ben can add one more show cooler (a horse blanket inscribed with the sponsor's logo) to his collection. As the spotlights come on and

Big Ben stands in the spotlight after winning the Grand Prix of Stuttgart.
(Jayne Huddleston)

the police band starts up, Ben rears, as he sometimes does during presentation ceremonies, then the Canadian national anthem is played, and the Canadian flag is lowered from the rafters. Ben and I lead the triumphal ride of winning horses and riders around the arena, but not before a European tradition is observed. The lights are dimmed and everyone flicks on the cigarette lighters that have been handed out by *Halle* staff minutes before. Thousands of tiny flames set against the darkness. What a beautiful sight!

In the press conference, I joke that while Big Ben's twenty-five owners will be very pleased, I am glad not to have to phone them all, because that would absorb all the prize money. Hans Pracht is another one pleased with our victory. He is later seen in the lounge of the Hotel Europe, enthusiastically waving Claus's 1,000-DM note.

That night as I drift off to sleep, my thoughts are on Big Ben and what an incredible horse he is. Sandi will give him his favourite snack — bran muffins. And when I am not looking (because I do not approve of spoiling horses — even super-stars), she will let Ben scratch his head on her back. He has earned his rewards. Horses may not know when they have lost; they do know when they have won.

In the morning we are off to the National Horse Show in New Jersey and the week after that to the Royal Winter Fair in Toronto. There is no time to rest on our laurels. The rider's rollercoaster speeds ever forward.

You are only as good as your last outing, and Stuttgart soon enough will be history. In New Jersey and Toronto, we will be expected to win. If we lose, there will be talk: Big Ben is washed up; Ian Millar is washed up. Staying at the top is even harder than getting there, which was hard enough.

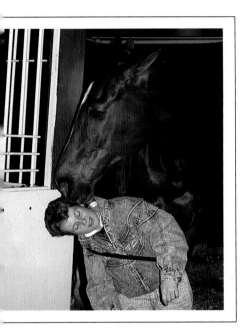

Big Ben playing with Sandi Patterson
(Suzanne Smith)

CHAPTER 2

Learning To Pull Up My Socks and Flicka

My mother remains, in her mid-seventies, alert and capable. Tiny but durable, she golfs in summer and in winter she cross-country skis from her country home in Montague, Prince Edward Island. Her memory is, like Doris Millar herself, formidable. One of her memories is of me sitting astride a piano bench at the age of five. I am wearing a cowboy hat, my six-guns are in their holsters, and my hands are pumping invisible reins. I am galloping. To where, I now wonder.

Eventually I would sit properly on that piano bench and learn to play the piano, but only after many years, and only because my mother was determined that I get my Grade 8 level in music. Her philosophy was a Maritime one: "What you start, you finish!" Perhaps I inherited her persistence. My passion, as I soon discovered, was for horses. It took hold

Lynn, my mother, Amy, Jonathon, and me on a cold day at Spruce Meadows
(Andy Rose)

and would not let go. Just as sure as God made little green apples, I was going to ride more than piano benches. Feeding my obsession with horses, and later, making a living by them, took all my considerable energy when the odds, good sense, and sometimes even my family, opposed it.

I was born Ian Donald Millar, on January 6, 1947, in Halifax. My father was Ian Adams Livingstone Millar, but everyone called him Liv. He was the son of a United Church minister, and his brother, my uncle, also became a minister. My father was born in Sackville, New Brunswick, and grew up in hard times. I remember him telling me that during the Depression the salary earned by my grandfather was meagre, and the congregation used to bring the family cakes and casseroles and other food. I don't remember a lot about my father's mother, but I am told that both she and my uncle were renowned storytellers who could keep a roomful of people spellbound. Perhaps I inherited a touch of that. Some say I tell a good story.

My father went to Dalhousie University dental school and worked during the summers in the coal mines of Springhill, Nova Scotia. After he graduated and began to practise dentistry, among the first things he bought were a bed, a dresser, and a bedside table, all of which he later gave to me and which I have since passed on to my son, Jonathon.

When the Second World War broke out, my father quit his private practice to join the Royal Canadian Dental Corps. He landed with the troops at D-Day and began to treat dental problems in soldiers, but also to perform facial surgery when the wounds centred on the mouth. He was an exceptional dentist. After the war, the Canadian army, fearing the loss of many good dentists, made it attractive for them to stay, and my father elected to remain in the army, eventually reaching the rank of colonel.

He had met my mother in London during the war. The daughter of a Maritime veterinarian, she was serving as a registered nurse in a wing of the armed forces known then as the No. 7 Royal Canadian General Hospital. A friend of hers was to be married and she was the bridesmaid; my father, a friend of the groom, was filling in for the best man. Two months later, in a typical wartime romance, Liv the best man and Doris the bridesmaid were themselves married.

My sister, Jeannie, was born the year the war ended. I came along two years later. My father's army job kept the family on the move, to Halifax, Washington, Victoria, and then, when I was five, to Ottawa, where I can recall my first memories.

Bruce Street, in the quiet west end of Ottawa, was home until I was ten. As a child I was not particularly bad; rambunctious was more like it.

But my father used to say I was accident-prone. Trouble seemed to follow me everywhere. I would always wonder, "Why me?"

I remember when I was about eight years old, sitting at our kitchen table, which was covered with a red-and-white chequered table cloth. The four of us were having a meal and I was fidgeting with the corner of the table cloth, which for some reason I had tied to my belt loop. My sister and I were at the stage where we always raced each other to answer the telephone. The instant it rang I leapt up to answer it. Needless to say, I was not like the magician who snaps out the table cloth leaving all the plates and glasses in place. *Everything* went with me.

Sometimes my misadventures were costly. We spent summers in Prince Edward Island, where my mother was born. One year, on our way, we stopped at a certain motel, and I was out throwing my ball against the side of the building near the neon sign showing the name of the motel. I hit the light and the whole sign went out. It was 7:00 P.M. on a summer evening and the unfortunate motel operator had no sign. My father deducted a percentage of my allowance for a long time to pay for that sign.

"It seemed like a good idea at the time" was my usual explanation for the things I did. I was the Beaver Cleaver of Bruce Street, who went after what he wanted: I needed a raccoon tail for my bike, but my parents were not prepared to buy me one, so I improvised. When I chanced upon a road-killed squirrel, I sawed off its tail and placed the tail between the inside and outside basement windows to dry. I promptly forgot it was there, leading in time to unspeakable odours, a proliferation of insects, and a predictable response from my parents.

A boy with a lot of energy, I was competitive and always wanted to play with older children. This combination offered ample opportunity for trouble. I remember a certain Firecracker Day when one of the older boys lit and threw a "cannon", as we called those big firecrackers, and it failed to go off. A group of us raced to retrieve it. I got there first, and as I picked up the cannon it blew backwards, lifting the skin right off my hand. I went home yowling and was in bandages for some time.

If it was not other boys I was racing, it was my sister — and she was fast, faster than me and probably still is. She later became a very fine middle-distance runner and one year came close to going to the Pan-American Games. Once when we were racing for the car Jeannie got there first and jumped in. I was trying to hold the door open; she was trying to close it. Not surprisingly, my finger got caught in the door. My parents arrived on the scene to find me screaming and my finger hanging by a piece of flesh. My father, at the tear, rushed me to the hospital where the doctors told him to forget about the end of my finger. It was gone. But my father insisted that the doctor sew it back on, thinking that if it did not take, it could be removed later. Thanks to his insistence and his knowledge of surgery, I have the end of my finger today. Works just fine. The loss of part of one digit would not have impaired my riding later on, but I'm grateful nevertheless.

The list of these childhood disasters goes on and on. My competitive nature meant that my young body was always taking a beating. In primary school I had a teacher who refused to let me out at recess: I threw myself into games with such vigour that she worried for my safety.

My sister was a very easy child for my parents; an honours student with an impeccable scholastic record. I was more difficult, an average student and a reluctant one at that. I was always being told, "Why can't you be more like your sister?" This did *not* have the desired effect. Yet Jeannie would always help me with my homework, despite my ungrateful lack of interest.

It is ironic that I came to be so robust. My life could have taken quite a different turn. When I was about five years old, I had contracted polio. This was in the early fifties, at the time of the epidemic. Except for feeling very lonely, I do not remember many details about the contagious-disease hospital in Ottawa where I spent a week. The drapes, my mother recalls, were all drawn. It was an awful place, with some of the children locked in iron lungs. I was allowed no contact with my family; only the telephone kept my parents informed.

When I arrived home I was made to stay for three weeks in a large crib placed in the dining room. A friend of the family—I called her "Auntie"—was a physiotherapist, and she came to the house to do exercises with me in the bathtub, my only escape from that crib. I did not want to straighten my leg; the exercises served to counter that tendency. I remember kicking like mad in the tub and sending water spilling over the side. The regular flooding of the bathroom floor apparently loosened ceiling tiles in the kitchen directly below, but that was the only legacy of my bout with polio.

My father was ambidextrous, and a brilliant handyman and technician. He spent evenings and weekends working on one project or another—finishing the basement, building a garage. He taught me many skills, such as carpentry, but I was not much interested. Slipping away was more my idea. His aim was to accomplish two goals at once: do something with the family, and especially his son, and get a project finished. He had great physical energy, which I inherited, and needed little sleep: six hours was enough. I do not remember him as athletic, but whatever he did—golf, curling, riding horses later on—he was good at it. My father was a dabbler.

I am often thankful for the sense of humour I inherited from my father.

   He had a wonderful sense of humour, but it was so subtle that half the time Jeannie and I did not realize when he was kidding, which was a source of frustration. I remember my mother constantly saying, "Ian, he's *teasing* you." I inherited that kind of humour, which I have tried to learn to control, because not everyone appreciates it. I tease the people I like, and the more I like them the more I am inclined to show my affection by teasing.

My father was not particularly religious, but he was a principled, ethical, correct person, just like my mother. I remember being with him and my sister at a store when the clerk gave him too much change. Dad realized it later, and he went back to return the change. Although I was only about six years old, I remember thinking at the time, "This is remarkable."

Soon after that I needed some colouring pencils for school. I went to the local Beamish store and found it was going to take my whole allowance to buy these pencils. No one was watching me, and I thought to myself, "If I walk out the door, I'll have my colouring pencils *and* my allowance." That struck me as a good idea, and I acted on it. That night it started to bother me. I was unable to sleep; I was upset; I was crying. My father came into my bedroom and asked me what was wrong. I told him what I had done.

"What do you think you should do about it?" he asked me.

"I have to go back there and pay for the pencils," I sobbed.

He nodded, "That's right."

The next day I went into the store, put the pencils on the counter, and paid for them.

The effect of these experiences on me was profound and long-lasting. In 1980, some twenty-seven years later, I was at a horse show at Lake Placid, New York. It was early in the morning, and for some reason I wanted lemonade. I bought some at a stand, and as I turned around to go, I saw a roll of money on the ground, amounting to about $400. I asked the lemonade seller who some of his customers had been that morning. I reasoned that there could not have been many; most people prefer coffee to lemonade in the morning. He described a few people, all horse people. One I recognized as Ray Little, an American acquaintance with whom I had once done some business. I wandered over to him.

I said, "Ray, I need to borrow $20."

"Sure," he said, and reached in his pocket. A look of shock came over his face.

"I don't know where my money is!"

I said, "I think I can help you out with that," and handed him the money.

During certain competitions, my honesty is put to the test. Mario Deslauriers and John Anderson were both my pupils, and I can remember many occasions when I rode in jump-offs and speed classes ahead of them. I was always very careful to tell them what I had learned from the ride. I essentially told them how to win it. I wore two hats — competitor and teacher — and felt compelled to convey to my students information that could spell my defeat. But now, years later, Mario will sometimes ride ahead of me in a jump-off and will pass on similar tips that could cost him a ribbon. And so, the debt is repaid.

Just spending time with horses, 1958

My father died quite suddenly in 1980 in his mid-sixties. I was in Prince Edward Island and had just finished teaching a riding clinic. He did not look well. After driving me to the airport, my mother convinced him to stop at the hospital, where he was diagnosed as having pneumonia. Four days later he was dead. It came as a terrible shock, and made me reflect more than I had before on the part my parents had played in my life.

Although a smoker all his life, my father had been healthy. In his retirement, he had been asked to help with a childrens' dental program in P.E.I.; always very good with people, and especially with children, he was practising part-time with my mother as his nurse. A smart and serious man, who set high standards for himself and the rest of the family, he was not easygoing nor particularly outgoing, but he was kind and compassionate. His legacy to me was his work habit and a sense of ethics that says, for example, that just because something is legal, it is not necessarily ethically correct.

My mother, on the other hand, passed on to me her own legacy — and is still doing so. Doris Millar is by nature and upbringing a determined woman. When I was about eight, my father was posted to Germany for a year, and during that period my mother looked after my sister and me by herself. She did it beautifully: she could be the loving supportive mother; she could also be the stern, authoritative figure.

When she started riding fairly late in life, she clearly possessed a natural talent, though she was more cautious and not as aggressive as my father. But from the minute the family started riding, she was nearly as interested in the whole business as I was. Through the years, she single-mindedly supported my riding. My father occasionally questioned the time and money going into the horses, but my mother was resolute that my interests and skills be developed. For this I will be eternally grateful.

That abiding interest existed from a very early age. It was when I was about five years old, and still riding make-believe horses on a piano bench, that I experienced my first contact with the real thing. Some people came around our neighbourhood with a pony wearing a western saddle; kids sat up on the pony and had their picture taken. My mother still has the picture of me somewhere. I was after my mother every time I saw that pony coming. By the time I was eight years old, my interest in horses had become an obsession. I watched westerns on television, and thought about horses a great deal.

At the time, horse-drawn wagons were still used to deliver milk, and I would be allowed to ride with the milkman for as many blocks as my parents and the milkman could tolerate. I was forever pestering my parents to let me ride; it was all I wanted to do. Finally, my father was put in charge of what the army called "western command". My parents said, "Look, Ian. We're moving to Edmonton. When we get to Edmonton you can ride."

I was convinced that as soon as we crossed the Manitoba border, there would be fewer cars and more horses, and as we progressed towards Alberta, there would finally be no cars and only horses. The West was the West. I had seen westerns on television; I knew how it was. My father would go to work on a horse, and I would go to school on a horse.

I cannot put into words how disappointed I was when it did not turn out that way.

A dentist friend of my father's had helped our family locate a cottage on Gull Lake, not far from Red Deer. We were to stay at the cottage for the summer, and my father would go to work in Edmonton and find us a house before September. As we approached the cottage, we passed a little store, and I saw two horses standing outside. A sign read "Horses to Rent". When we arrived, I immediately jumped out of the car and ran back to the store as fast as I could go. I wanted to know all about this.

There were two options: it cost a dollar for an hour's ride, or twenty-five cents to go down the road a hundred yards on one of two horses named Socks and Flicka and then ride back. I ran home, tried for the dollar, could not get it, and settled for a quarter.

I got up on Socks, a slim-built four-year-old chestnut with high withers (the protruding bone at the base of the horse's neck, just ahead of where a saddle would go). Riding bareback, I walked down to the end of the road with him because that is all I could coax him to do: he did not want to leave the other horse. Then I turned him around (I had seen westerns, remember, I knew what to do), gave him a kick, and he trotted. But I felt that was rough, so I gave him another kick and a cluck and he cantered back to the store. I thought this was wonderful. My first

One of my first mounts (right) at Gull Lake, 1957

real ride — and I immediately went home. . . . This time I did manage to extricate a dollar from my parents; now I had an hour.

A seventeen-year-old farm boy in the area ran the enterprise. He would bring his horses to the general store and people would rent them. Soon I was grooming the horses and getting them water. I would be there all day. Next I began to look after the business when the older boy was busy with farm chores. I would rent the horses out, and my pay was freedom to ride them when they were not working.

At night local people who had horses would come over to the store and eight or ten of us would all go out riding around the cottages and in the fields. It was all heady stuff for a ten-year-old, because these people — they were probably sixteen or seventeen — seemed so much older. I was the only young one they accepted into this inner circle because I worked for the ring-leader of the whole gang. He took me under his wing.

We would get on those horses and gallop up and down the sand roads around the lake. Never a saddle. Sissies used saddles.

I was as happy as any ten-year-old boy on the planet. I had found my Wild West after all.

What was it about horses that so captivated me, a city boy who had seen only a few real horses? Perhaps my passion for horses was simply inborn: I was lucky enough to discover it at a very early age. I can still recall my first gallop on Socks. I had never been more comfortable or happier in my whole life. Galloping at the age of ten, during my first moments on a horse: those are normally the ingredients for a nasty fall. But I did not fall; I had this God-given gift. It was a tremendous feeling to be on that horse, to be part of him. I enjoyed the gallop, when he pushed with his hind end, reached out with his front end, and his body crouched low to the ground. Bareback you could feel the ribs, the muscles, the back; you could feel it all. Even now I still love the feel of a horse galloping under me.

Later I would fall while galloping, fall repeatedly. One day a group of us were galloping along a sandy road. Whatever horse I was on turned into a laneway leading to a cottage. Just made a sudden turn. I, of course, kept going straight, and landed right on my face and stomach. It took the hide off me. I was embarrassed falling off in front of everybody. But I made no noise, retrieved the horse, got back on, and away I went again.

It was not only riding I loved, but anything to do with those horses. I would have been content to stand there and brush them all day. Or just pat them. Because by now, at the age of ten, I was focused. And the focus was horses.

CHAPTER 3

The Luck of the Draw

Luck runs like a theme through my life. Luck brought me to my best mount, Big Ben, and at precisely the right moment. I have always had luck, and in my sport you need it. In a show-jumping event, good luck will keep a rail up, even when your horse has hit it hard; bad luck will bring the same rail down when your horse has barely rubbed it. One fence up or down at an event such as the du Maurier International at Spruce Meadows, the show-jumping tournament in Calgary, can mean a difference of $65,000 if that rail separates first from second place.

On Brandywine in Mrs. Gardiner's paddock, summer of 1959

When I was ten years old and possessed by thoughts of horses, I had the good luck to encounter fine teachers. I owe them a great deal, and they deserve a special place in this book. At Mrs. Gardiner's School of Riding in Edmonton, I learned principles of horsemanship that remain with me today. By the time I was twelve I was being tutored by a German dressage rider at that stable in Olympic-level dressage techniques. This was doctorate material being taught a pupil in Grade 5.

No doubt I possessed natural riding talent. My great good fortune, though, was to connect with knowledgeable people who recognized that talent and set about to shape it.

Throughout the summer of 1957, thanks to Socks and Flicka, I had sores and blisters on my backside. My mother would say, "You have to stop riding and let these things get better." But I was not about to stop.

We moved to Edmonton that fall, and I dragged the family to riding lessons every Saturday morning at Rita Gardiner's School of Riding. (The school no longer exists and Mrs. Gardiner passed away several years ago.) Mrs. Gardiner was very, very serious, so much so that she intimidated most people. We thought she dressed unusually — bandannas on her head, hair going every which way, always jodhpurs and felt riding-boots. Always. She was a painter, and I still have some of her paintings. But she was in the barn most of the time, and the house — which no one cleaned much — was full of cats and dogs. Not much else mattered but horses.

At Mrs. Gardiner's we learned to groom and tack up ("tack" is the general term for saddles and bridles), to mount the horse, lead the horse, and walk around the ring. That was the first lesson. But I found this enormously frustrating: I thought I knew all that. Worse, we were using a sissy English saddle, without a horn, and were holding the reins one in each hand. I rode with the reins in *one* hand.

Nevertheless, I was thrilled to be there. Of course I wanted more than just a weekly lesson, but my parents declared that I would have to pay for any additional lessons. I needed work, and I found it: I had a paper route, I sold magazines, I worked as a caddy at the golf course, I cut grass and shovelled snow, driving the neighbours crazy. My business ventures had but one aim — to raise money for more riding. (Or at least, that was the theory. Being a caddy stirred a brief interest in golf. One day, while the neighbours were vacationing and I was supposed to be minding their house, keeping the grass trimmed and the indoor plants watered, I put a golf ball through their picture window and a great hole in my summer earnings.) This was the beginning of a continuing link in my life between business and riding. Until I could raise capital, there would be no extra riding, and the riding used up lots of capital. I leapt on that merry-go-round when I was ten years old, and I have been on it ever since.

Mrs. Gardiner (adults called her Lou) saw my interest. She had me muck the stalls, groom the horses, help with the hay — all in exchange for more riding. My sister and I were streamed off to ride with a group of ten- to twelve-year-olds. In no time I could do everything that they could do, although they had been riding for several years. By the time I was eleven, I was teaching eight- and nine-year-olds how to groom, how to clean out a horse's feet, and how to tack up.

With Mrs. Gardiner and Lil and Dixie

Once you were proficient enough in the ring, your reward from Mrs. Gardiner was to ride the horse in a walk out in the field. I remember one occasion when we were all riding out in the field and I was on an older pony called Swannie. Mrs. Gardiner was afoot. Swannie saw a puddle, trotted over, walked right into the middle, and flopped down. As she rolled over, I stepped off. I was quite sure that Swannie was dying. Mrs. Gardiner was screaming at the top of her lungs, "Don't you let that pony do that!" I didn't know it, but this was one of Swannie's big tricks — rolling in puddles. I was absolutely mortified.

But the experience was part of a valuable lesson. Mrs. Gardiner taught me this: "It's never the horse's fault." New riders, even some experienced riders, want to blame the horse. A student would say, "The horse doesn't want to leave the barn," and Mrs. Gardiner would counter, "It's your fault because you're not doing [this or that] correctly." And, for the most part, I would agree that the horse is usually not at fault.

Mrs. Gardiner taught me always to look to myself first and to examine everything I could have done. Today, it would be easy to say after a fine round with only one rub and four faults that the horse just did not jump high enough at one fence. It has been my way — no doubt Mrs. Gardiner was an influence — to say, "What could I have done differently?" I will study the videotape of that ride, replay it over and over again. Sometimes it *is* the horse; but many times I am to blame.

At the riding school some of us came to the conclusion that, if your balance were good, there was no need for a girth (the band around the horse securing the saddle). We therefore set out to ride with a saddle but no girth. This was fine on the flat. And if — we continued on this line of thinking — your balance were *really* good, you should be able to *jump* without a girth. We started. We made the jumps a little bigger, then bigger still. I was the daredevil in testing this theory. Finally my horse took a jump and the saddle and I went flying. I landed on my side with the saddle underneath me. It was a long time before my hip forgave me. To this point I had been sure I was indestructible and that accidents always happened to other people. I now knew otherwise.

I have heard of no one else doing this, but Mrs. Gardiner used to teach us to fall off a horse. (This practice was reserved for younger riders only.) We would be walking along on horseback and she would say, "Now fall off." And we did. She would muck the contents of the stalls — mainly shavings and dried manure — into the riding area. With such a cushion, it was like falling on a pillow. Another exercise involved riding into the paddock with just halters and ropes on our horses (no saddles), and pulling all the other riders off their horses. The last one on a horse was the winner. Falling off a horse came to be no big deal at all.

Mrs. Gardiner also taught us respect for the horse. In her eyes the horse was the king, and we were all there to serve the king; we were to feel fortunate and privileged to be associated with such a noble animal. It was not hard to teach me that because I basically had felt it from the beginning.

In one of her early lessons she taught us horse etiquette, such as how to pat a horse. She said, "You walk up to him and you pat him on the shoulder, and if he turns his head towards you, if he seems to want it done, pat him on the face." She made the point splendidly by example. She turned to someone nearby, took her hand and patted that individual on the forehead and the nose. And of course the person stepped back. She then said, "And how did you like that? Would you have preferred that someone pat you on the shoulder?"

To this day, when I see someone go up to a horse and pat him on the face, I always watch the horse to see his reaction. Some just tolerate it, but you can tell by their look and the position of their ears that they do not enjoy it.

With Lil and Dixie

Mrs. Gardiner was a brilliant teacher of basic horsemanship. She taught principles and ideas as well as techniques. In the hunter/jumper world today so many people teach just technique. The riders they teach become technically masterful riders who view their horses as machines. They lack the ability to feel what each horse is all about. They have been taught skills, but not horsemanship. Imagine a world-class race-car driver who does not know how to open a car's hood.

Mrs. Gardiner's husband, Bert, was more of a farmer/rancher type who took care of the nuts-and-bolts operation of the riding school. While she taught me the more sophisticated and stylish approach to horses, he taught me the cowboy approach: how to trim a horse's foot, how to nail on a shoe. He had decided I was all right, and he talked to me a great deal about farming and breaking horses. An old cowboy friend of his taught us about trick-roping and Roman riding, which involves standing up on one moving horse or sometimes two horses at once, a foot on each rump.

Mrs. Gardiner was the one delegated to deal with riders and the public; Bert was the strong, silent type in the background. With my sandwiches in a brown paper bag, I would join him for lunch. He and I loved to play horseshoes at noon with the other men on the farm. To this day I throw a good horseshoe.

A doctor of internal medicine, Dr. Otto Bode, boarded horses at Mrs. Gardiner's. He was of her vintage, in his sixties. Dressage was his passion. He was always dressed correctly in breeches and boots, neat as a pin. Dr. Bode was strict, sober; I never saw him laugh. He was a hard, hard worker, very German: there was a way to do everything according to a system, a structure, a discipline. At the time, however, the concept of "a system" eluded me. That appreciation was to come later, from another teacher, to whom, along with all the others, I owe so much.

Dr. Bode and Mrs. Gardiner decided that I could be his assistant. During the fall, winter, and spring Dr. Bode rode Tuesdays and Thursdays after work and every Saturday and Sunday morning; during the summer he rode six mornings a week. The Germans are reputed to be the best in the world at dressage, which they invented, and he was from the old German school. He believed that the horse would learn when the horse was ready to learn, and that was a great lesson for me. Patience is the key. Knowing *when* is just as important as *how*. This understanding would take me many years to develop. Not only with horses, but with people.

I took the bus to Dr. Bode's office, drove out to the riding school with him, and got his horses ready. He lunged them — trained them to obey his voice commands — "walk", "trot", "canter", "whoa" — while they circled around him at the end of a long line. This taught them balance on a circle, stride control, and obedience. It was not long before he said, "You should sit on these horses while I lunge them." I did — without reins or stirrups. Then he had me juggle tennis balls while I was on the horses, or ride facing backwards, or with both legs on one side. I now know that he was teaching *me* balance while teaching the horse balance. Soon I did not think about balance; it came naturally.

Dr. Bode was a master, a slow, methodical, and patient trainer. He told me where to put my legs and hands; he gave me a series of actions to perform so he could observe the horse. But he never explained the why of it all. I am sure that what he did say was dry; I remember him droning on about the correctness of the trot. But years later, when I was twenty-one, I found myself doing something with my body while riding a horse and getting the right result. How did I know to do that? Dr. Bode gave me those tools without ever teaching me when they were to be used. He had a certain military bearing, and it was not the style then for teachers to offer theory to their students.

Dr. Otto Bode, a master of dressage, who taught me a great deal.

But what unbelievable luck! I was a boy riding what I perceived to be Olympic-class dressage horses, and getting two and a half years of concentrated education. I had talent and enthusiasm, and good teachers were drawn to that. Both Dr. Bode and Mrs. Gardiner were tough, though. There were no indoor arenas in those days. Regardless of the temperature outside, hot or cold, their thinking was that if you really wanted to do this thing, you made up your mind and concentrated on it. I thought that was just fine. I never questioned it.

I remember one of my first competitions — a breeding show in Wetaskiwin, Alberta. Mrs. Gardiner had bred a certain Appaloosa, and the event meant a great deal to her. Only one student would go, and when I was selected, I realized what an honour it was. I won the "best showmanship" prize for showing the horse on the line. In this class the horse isn't ridden at all, but is led by his handler so that judges can observe the horse's movement and evaluate his conformation. I still have the trophy. Another time, when I was fourteen, I went with Dr. Bode to a dressage show, and, with me in the saddle, we won everything against much older riders — handily. The wins had little to do with me, however. Dr. Bode, who was then light years ahead of anyone else in the area, had simply trained his horses better than the rest.

In the summer we went four or five times to the shows, which were one-day affairs. There were English and western classes, and we would do both, trading English riding hats and jodhpurs for chaps and cowboy hats, English saddles for western ones, according to the class we were in. There were gymkhana events — the three-legged race, the sack race, the egg-and-spoon race — all combined with pony riding. We also competed in barrel-racing and pole-bending events (like slalom racing in skiing). It was a well-rounded education I got in riding, and it was fun too.

When I was fifteen, my father was transferred back to Ottawa. The family had by this time owned two horses. The first was called Brandy-wine. He was a family horse — my mother rode him during the week, my father rode him western, and my sister and I would share him on the weekends. The horse could do tricks. He could count, kneel (so I could get on him), rear, all in the Gene Autry style. I have a mental picture of my father wearing a cowboy hat and sitting on a western saddle; when he gave this big, tall horse a light tug on the mouth, Brandywine would stand up on his hind legs and rear.

We later sold Brandywine and bought Bonnie Dundee, a Palomino. He was an extraordinarily versatile horse. When news came of my father's transfer, we decided to bring Bonnie Dundee back to Ottawa with us, and that decision led to another: I would cross the country in a boxcar of a train with the horse. When my mother thinks back to it, she wonders whatever possessed her to allow it.

This was the summer of 1962. In those days moving companies made it their business to know who was moving and then to contact the family. Some firms called us, but as soon as my mother told them we were moving a horse too, they suddenly lost interest. However, one enterprising mover read a Canadian Pacific rulebook that said you could move "goods and chattel" in a railway car. If you had so many pounds of furniture, you got the whole car. So the Millars rented a railway car. The furniture was packed at each end, and in the middle a stall was built for Bonnie Dundee and a cot was set up for me. With me was Ruggles, the family cocker spaniel, my guitar, a radio, a coolerful of food for the five-day journey, and — just in case I ran out of food — a case of chocolate and vanilla Metrecal, that meal-in-a-can liquid for dieters.

The railway-car doors were nailed open a foot or two and held in place by a board at chest height, because I was then something of a sleepwalker, and because, unless the doors were secured, they opened and closed with the rocking of the train.

My parents and sister flew back east. "See you in Ottawa," we said to each other. This was great adventure. At each whistle stop I would wave to everyone. But soon the adventure went a little sour — literally. Milk spilled in the cooler and spoiled all my food, including a roast. I had to drink the Metrecal, which I despised. At one station I bought a wooden case — twenty-four bottles in all — of Orange Crush, which I lived on for two and a half days. Only in the last few years have I been able to face Orange Crush again; my stomach for Metrecal is beyond rescue. The ride, too, was rougher than I anticipated; a freight train does not ride like a passenger train. While I was sound asleep one night, my aluminum cot collapsed from all the jarring.

One day we were pulling out of a little place somewhere on the prairie, and I was waving to the station master, when I heard a noise behind me. Two men, hoboes, were about to climb in the other side of my freight car. I was afraid they would steal everything and throw me out, and then who would look after my horse and my dog? I appealed to people on the platform to stop the train, but they yelled back that it was too late.

One hobo asked, "Can we get a ride?"

I told him, "No!"

He said, "Ah, come on!" and started to climb in. He had placed his fingers on the wooden crossboard. I had with me as weapons a pitchfork and a ball-peen hammer, and I gave him a crack on the fingers with the hammer. He let go, fell backwards, and landed on his companion, who was running along behind. I was petrified that they had gotten on another car and would climb forward to visit me, but I never saw them again.

The only other incident occurred in Winnipeg. The railway yard there is in Transcona, and is the biggest one in Canada, covering many, many square miles. Bonnie Dundee was sick. He had a little discharge from his nose; he was looking dull, not drinking or eating. I had to find a vet. Climbing over and under endless rows of trains, I finally came to a little shack, and I told the fellow there that my horse was sick. He gave me a questioning stare, but when I explained further, he agreed to call a vet.

I had no idea how much time remained before my train was connected to an eastbound train leaving Transcona, and when I arrived back to find the train gone, I felt genuine panic. Gone as well was my money, which I had left in the boxcar. (Lesson learned. I would never again leave my wallet behind anywhere.) I found the shack again, and the railwayman saw by his board that the train had in fact not departed but had only been moved to another track. He found it for me again. My boxcar was as I had left it, and late that night, while I was sleeping, a vet appeared and told me that my horse had shipping fever, a stress-related lung and throat condition. He gave him antibiotics, I paid him, and off we went again.

Somewhere in northern Ontario it started to pour. Rain was sweeping in the open door. I woke up and my sleeping bag was drenched; I was shaking like a leaf from the cold. In the middle of the night, we finally reached Ottawa, and my mother and father climbed into the railway car and woke me up. I was *so* glad to see them! Bonnie Dundee was put in a truck and taken to the farm of someone who had been recommended to us: Nancy Woods at Lucerne, Quebec, just outside Ottawa.

This would be the start of a new phase in my life. From Nancy Woods and her husband, John (later to be the best man at my wedding) I learned a great deal. But by now I was a teenager, getting difficult, rebellious, cocky on a horse. I thought I knew it all. I had a lot to learn.

Deciding they wanted property in the country, my parents bought twenty-five acres of land next to the Woodses' stables and built a house. Thanks to our family riding lessons in Edmonton, my mother had begun to share something of my own passion for horses, and, at age forty, she began to teach riding, which she would do for more than ten years. (In fact, she was sixty-five before she *quit* riding.) My father and I built a small barn with four stalls, plus a one-horse trailer. We had Bonnie Dundee and three other horses at home, I was taking lessons with Mrs. Woods, and before long I was working for her teaching young riders.

Nancy Woods was tall, blonde, and slim. Always nattily dressed, she had a husky voice and smoked thin cigars. She was like Mrs. Gardiner in some ways: she was hard-working and eccentric. Whether the horse business creates such eccentrics or attracts them is hard to say; what is certain is that the horse world teems with them. Both Mrs. Gardiner and Nancy Woods loved horses, and considered that, if you cut any corner, the injured party was the horse — a circumstance neither would tolerate. It did not take much to get either one of them mad at you. One day I was mucking the stalls at the Woodses' stable. Nancy came in, took the wheelbarrow full of manure, and flipped it upside down in the stall. "That's not good enough," she said. Another time she threw a hammer at me, but missed.

As teachers, Mrs. Gardiner and Nancy Woods would brook no shortcuts, no insults to horses. Today, neither do I.

Before long I was spending every waking hour at Nancy Woods's stable. She bought and sold horses and did the flatwork (the basic training of horses). I did the jumping work. Like many in the horse business, she had clients who owned horses but who needed help with their training. Some clients' horses needed a strong, aggressive ride occasionally, because they had learned bad habits. My job was to straighten them out. Nancy taught me equitation and I began to enter equitation classes, in which only the rider is judged on his or her form — body, leg, and hand position, as well as riding skills — not the horse. At the age of seventeen, I became her partner. From Nancy I learned about jumping, barn management, the horse business in general. Very quickly I soaked this all up. What I was slow to learn was patience.

I was a young adult who thought he had it all figured out. I was independent, belligerent about being told what to do, and not always easy to instruct. Nancy would watch me trying to teach a horse something, and of course I wanted the horse to absorb the lesson right away. She would say, "Ian, you don't have any sympathy for that horse." This infuriated me.

"What do you mean, 'I don't have sympathy'? I'm asking this horse to do a perfectly simple thing and he won't do it. The horse is being unreasonable. I'm not being unreasonable." It took me three years to learn what Nancy meant by the word *sympathy* (*empathy* is more accurate), but that hard lesson was also the most valuable, and I will always be grateful for it: the ability to see life through a horse's eyes.

At home I was still rebellious. Job offers to ride were coming in and exerting a real pull, because school held no interest at all for me. My parents, on the other hand, were determined that I get an education. By sheer force of my mother's will, I had completed my Grade 8 piano (worth a Grade 13 academic credit), and I would indeed need to play that card to slip the surly bonds of high school: I had come up a little short in chemistry.

All I wanted to do was ride in every class in every horse show. Nancy Woods and the horse world were coming between my family and me.

In those days, competitive show jumping was more the concern of the elite. There was the Ottawa Country Club, there were definite social classes, and, according to Nancy, riders were supposed to aspire to the higher classes. She wondered out loud why my father had stayed in the army and taken — as she saw it — the safe, secure way instead of getting out into private practice, where there was more money and where wise investments would lead to more affluence, allowing the family to acquire more and better horses. Such criticism of my parents bothered me a great deal. John Woods, the son of an old and prestigious Ottawa family, argued that it was not so much the education you got at a private school that was important, it was the chance to meet people who would become your business associates later in life. Business, business, business. Whereas my father might talk to me about becoming a dentist or a professional, Nancy Woods believed that education was unnecessary. The Woodses were sketching one kind of future for me, while my parents stood for something else.

I came home with the Woodses' ideas, and I even became judgemental about my parents. The result was strained relations between my parents and John and Nancy Woods. I was caught in the middle. I survived by walking a tightrope, but I learned that blood is indeed thicker than water.

The show-jumping world has long been criticized for its exclusivity; ordinary people, it is said, have no entry into what someone once called "the royal jelly of sports". That was even more true when I was a teenager in the mid-sixties, and I began to feel uncomfortable and insecure in this elitist environment. Since then I have come to realize that "high" society is no higher or better, but no worse either, than less affluent society. Just different. The idea of me as a teenager being coached in how to behave in "society" strikes me now as ludicrous. Surely I should be comfortable and natural talking to anyone, no matter what their status or professional rank? And indeed, now I am.

What is true in show jumping, however, is that to be successful you need great horses; you therefore need financial resources of your own or support from other people. I have found that the latter method can bring an unexpected bonus: many of my owners and investors bring to our partnership a special knowledge and understanding of horses and of the sport in general.

But I regret as a young man feeling any dissatisfaction with my parents, or thinking any less of them. It was all very selfish on my part, because my parents were absolutely supportive. They simply made me work for what I got.

Work. That was the problem. After graduating from high school in Nepean, Ontario, my rebellious streak continued, but my mania for horses had bred in me a practical streak as well. I realized that if my parents' support of my obsession was to continue, I would have to compromise and agree to their request that I further my education. A diploma in business administration seemed just the ticket. At the Eastern Ontario Institute of Technology in Ottawa (later called Algonquin College), my fellow students were older than I was, some of them married and back in school after years in the work force. While my other friends were getting degrees in commerce at university and taking a more intellectual approach, I was rubbing shoulders with some hardened veterans of the bottom line.

I was twenty-three when I graduated in the spring of 1970. By then I had met Lynn Doran.

She was a rider too, and was based at the John R. Allen stable a few miles from the Woods stable. She was dating my best friend, but he had told me that it was only a relationship of convenience because neither

had a particular boyfriend or girlfriend. Regularly, I would ride my horse over to the Allen stable, and hang out there. One night the three of us were at Lynn's place. At one point Lynn and I found ourselves alone together, and something clicked. Things were never the same again.

Now the problem of breaking this news to my best friend presented itself. Lynn was, and still is, very direct, but when we told him he was not pleased, despite what he had told me earlier. All he said was, "At least make the loss of our friendship worth it. Marry Lynn."

This was in May. After our third date, Lynn and I agreed on a September wedding. Ours was a feverish romance, and though neither of us had had any real plans to marry, we became convinced that this was what we both wanted most.

Lynn, who by this time had done some world travelling and acquired a degree in nursing, had a broad interest in all horse matters: riding, teaching, horse care, breeding, training, buying, and selling. Lynn's passion for horses by no means paled beside mine. She became more and more involved with Nancy Woods and the horses that Nancy and I were working on. There was never any question that horses would be our life; the questions were how, and when.

Lynn's father was a good man, but a tough one who owned his own construction firm. John Woods told me, "You can't marry Hugh Doran's daughter if you don't have a job. How would you like to be a stockbroker?"

With my fellow students in New York, learning to be a stockbroker. I am second from the right in the front row.

"It's as good as anything," I told him, "because I don't want to do anything but ride."

Shortly after, John helped arrange an interview with a New York-based firm called Thomson & McKinnon Auchincloss Inc. (Hugh Auchincloss was the stepfather of Jackie Kennedy and gave her away when she married John F. Kennedy.) I remember I had to write tests to determine my suitability for the company. The manager called me back in after the tests and said, "The tests indicate you will have three jobs, which you honestly believe are your career jobs, before the age of twenty-seven. You won't settle to one career until then. And it will cost us a lot [about $20,000, if I remember correctly] to train you. You're a bad bet. But I'm going to hire you anyway." That was also probably courtesy of John Woods.

The training was extensive. It meant completing a three-month correspondence course, going to the office each day in Ottawa, and then spending three months in New York City at head offices on Wall Street. There I learned a lot – including the salesman's trick of quickly memorizing the names of my fifty fellow students. Meanwhile, I had married Lynn, who was busy working at the Woods farm, training horses and giving lessons, and was also working part-time as a private-duty nurse. We competed at show-jumping events on the weekend.

I had a starting income of $500 a month. Our payments for the little A-frame house we had bought in Wychwood, Quebec (complete with a dog named Moochie), the car loan, and other expenses, all came to $1,200 a month. This was my introduction to financial stress. Boarding horses and competing in the show ring were not helping any, because the prize money was hardly pouring in, and in those days it counted for little anyway. Sometimes a horse deal would put us temporarily in the black; otherwise we were very much in the red. I had to find another job if we were to continue with horses, let alone feed ourselves. With luck I had found the job as a stockbroker; with luck I would find another one. But where?

CHAPTER 4

Earning a Degree in Matters Equine

To rescue me from my financial distress came an unlikely saviour: the Canadian Broadcasting Corporation.

Someone from CBC Radio had asked if the brokers in our office wanted to do a statistical market report just before six every evening. It was decided that those brokers in the office who wanted to do this would take turns on an afternoon show, "Now, Just Listen", hosted by Elizabeth Gray. After we had all taken our turns for a few weeks, Mike Maltby, the executive producer of the show, came to our office to see the manager and I was called in. It seems that the CBC did not like my colleagues; for some reason, they liked me.

On Warrior
(Andy Rose)

The CBC had decided that it wanted daily commentary as well as statistics: three minutes of commentary, two minutes of statistics. Would I like to do this at $25 each time, or $125 a week? This would mean I would be close to meeting our expenses at home. I said, "Absolutely!"

The CBC Radio studios were on the seventh floor of the stately Château Laurier Hotel in Ottawa, about an eight-minute walk from our offices. Daily at five to six the producer hustled me into the studio, I sat down at the table, and Elizabeth introduced me.

"And now we have Ian D. Millar on the markets."

"Good evening, Elizabeth."

"Good evening, Ian, how are the markets?"

And away I went for five minutes – unless she or the producer were bored that day. On those occasions Elizabeth would get this gleam in her eye and would interrupt me with some obscure question that she had dug out of the financial pages: "I noticed International Widgets was down two points today. Do you know why, Ian?" Well, I had usually never *heard* of International Widgets, but I eventually learned to relax and to assure Elizabeth that I would have an answer for her the next day.

Soon, the CBC Radio morning show wanted me to do the same thing, for three minutes at $15 per broadcast. This could be done on the telephone from our home at 7:57 A.M. Now Lynn and I were in the black. We had it made.

My part-time career in radio would last just over a year. Ahead for me in the 1970s lay some of life's great adventures: the births of our son, Jonathon, and our daughter, Amy; participation in two Olympic Games; the dizzying acquisition and gut-wrenching loss of a real-estate portfolio; crippling debt; and a sometimes thorny, often fortuitous, path that by 1980 would take me to where I wanted to be – solvent, independent, and riding good horses.

But this was all to come. In 1971, when I was not selling stocks or doing stints on the radio, I was on a horse. Lynn and I would sometimes go to horse shows on a Thursday evening, and on Friday morning I would file my market report from wherever I was – a motel, a pay phone. The CBC's roving reporter.

By this time, Nancy Woods and I had discovered a grand prix horse, a grey called War Machine. He was a difficult, ornery animal – half thoroughbred and half who knows what – who had not worked out for other people. He was by far the best horse I had ridden to that point.

I had been on some wild and woolly horses. During my college days I had bought, from a farmer near Ottawa, a stallion called Sailor King, by a thoroughbred out of a standardbred mare. Standardbreds make wonderful trotters and pacers, but they tend not to canter very well, and in show jumping we use the canter—a slow, controlled gallop—a great deal. Thoroughbreds, bred to gallop and race, are much more suitable for show jumping. Using a standardbred in the show ring is unusual.

Sailor King's parentage did not bode well, but I bought him anyway, and I renamed him High Roller. Half standardbred and half thoroughbred, he was thoroughly crazy. I had scraped together a $400 loan to buy him—$200 from Nancy Woods and $200 from a fellow student named Allan Baker who worked part-time in his father's paint store.

I arrived at the farmer's place, and there was the horse, wild, skinny, nervous, and refusing to get in the trailer.

"I'll get him in the trailer," the farmer said knowingly. He got a long rope and put it around the horse's neck. Then he ran the rope in through the trailer, over the chest bar, out the front, and finally past and back out behind the horse. He then hooked the rope onto the back of his tractor, threw the tractor into gear, and slowly drove away.

The horse, understandably, resisted; had this been an animated cartoon it might have been funny. His front legs were back underneath him and he was literally dragged into the trailer on his knees and his nose. I was horrified and should have realized then that the horse had been abused, that his ability to be trained had been compromised. He was a worrier; you could keep no weight on him.

Sure enough, High Roller could not canter very well, but he could jump. My mother, for some reason, named him Finnegan, and that became his barn name. I did, in fact, do some amazing things on High Roller.

When I took him to a horse show at Expo '67, the world's fair in Montreal, it was really a case of the twenty-year-old country boy entering the big leagues. We competed in the preliminary division of this important show. The major players from all over Canada were there, plus some Americans. I was going to show them what this was all about. At one point on the course there were two oxers thirty-six feet apart. (Also called spread fences, oxers comprise two or more rails, walls, or gates, placed to create a wide jump, thus testing the horse's power.) This combination jump requires two strides: a horse should take two strides in thirty-six feet, one stride in twenty-four feet. My strategy was brazen: get going fast enough to cover the distance in one stride and save a second. Well, nobody does that. Occasionally horses will cover thirty-four feet between *vertical* jumps in one stride, but never thirty-six feet between *oxers* in one stride. I wound up at the end of the field, hell-bent for that jump. The gods must have been with me, because somehow we jumped it just right. The crazed High Roller jumped out in one stride, and we won the class. Ridiculous.

In those days I gambled like mad. Many of my big wins came from defying the odds. Today I still gamble, and at times I am just as aggressive, but I have learned when to gamble, and when it would be foolish. I have become more calculating, a percentage gambler.

We had another horse called Bull's Eye. Nancy Woods and I first saw him at the Mountain Road Riding Centre in Lucerne, Quebec. He belonged to a western rider who rode him with a large bit. For weekend entertainment at the riding school, he would jump the horse over his convertible car. When Bull's Eye was later moved to another stable we went to see him there. He was in a standing stall, which is much narrower than a box stall; wound around his neck was a thick chain and a padlock. It seems the western rider had not paid his bills, so we got the horse by paying his back board — $250. Bull's Eye was a bargain, but he was determined *not* to be trained. He had lots of power, but he was too brave, too aggressive, too hot. Never a careful horse, Bull's Eye would aim low and hit hard. He actually *broke* quite a few jumps, which somehow never seemed to embarrass me. Off we would go to shows and we would break the jumps. I was sure that Bull's Eye was going to work out. He did not.

With difficult, reject horses such as High Roller and Bull's Eye, Lynn and I were finally in the horse business. We were weekend gypsies. Before we got married, my means of conveying horses to shows had been a small two-horse trailer pulled slowly — and up hills very slowly — by an even smaller four-speed Austin Cambridge. Later, Lynn and I got a truck to pull the trailer. Finally, we bought a six-horse van. We would get to the competition, put the horses in the show barn, then clean out the trailer and set up house in it. We had a kerosene stove, a couple of cots as beds, and a cooler with ice as a fridge. At the shows, that was home.

By 1971, then, we had War Machine. He was big enough — 16.3 or 17 hands — and we had high hopes for him, but in today's competitive jumping he would be little more than a top amateur horse or an international rider's "second horse", one who specializes in the speed and novelty classes rather than grand prix events. Show jumping has changed a great deal in the past ten to fifteen years. It has gone from a sport that did not allow riders to make a living to one in which riders can do quite well financially. A horse like War Machine today would command a price of $30,000 to $50,000 — just because he had a small talent for jumping.

Nancy Woods did a superb job on his flatwork. My job was to get him in range of the jump; once he got in range, he was talented, very brave and resourceful. And he jumped the jumps. In the beginning, his evasion — his method of resisting being taught — was to take the bit and run. I would take him on drag hunts (done with hounds and on horseback, but in pursuit of a dragged scent as opposed to a real fox), and

On War Machine

the trick was to stop War Machine from passing the field master, which was considered poor etiquette. Eventually War Machine realized that his evasion did not bother me, and he stopped using it. Early in his career we won the Sutton Grand Prix in southern Ontario.

Meanwhile, I had been noticed. I had been scouted by the national team the year before and was invited to join. The national team — chosen from a pool of up to twelve riders — comprises the top five Canadian riders who have competed at certain designated shows throughout the year to gain a place on the team. Individual success at these shows now translates into points, but at times in the past, team members have been selected on a subjective basis. Each year, new team members are chosen.

Various combinations of these twelve riders represent Canada in the four Nations' Cup, or team, events held annually at the four international shows in North America. There are many more Nations' Cups in Europe, and at the end of the year, the team amassing the most points in all Nations' competitions world-wide is awarded a prestigious trophy. However, to date the Canadian team has never campaigned to win the trophy. Teams that will represent Canada at the Pan-American Games, the Olympic Games, and World Championships are also selected from the list of twelve riders. Only on these occasions does the team ride as a team; on all other occasions, team members continue to compete as individuals.

There had been talk in 1971 that the team was difficult to penetrate, but just by virtue of competing in Toronto and doing well enough in grand prix competitions, I was invited to join. However, a horseman we knew in Toronto, a former cavalry officer in the Polish army named Lou Mikucki, advised us that War Machine was too inexperienced for the fall circuit. We heeded that advice and did not go.

Nonetheless, things were falling into place. Doug Cudney, who had been on the Canadian show-jumping team before becoming its chairman, took a shine to me. His family always had horses. Doug authorized one of his employees (Bob Maron, who was also the team's *chef d'équipe*) to buy War Machine from us for $25,000, which was a lot of money then. They would keep me as War Machine's rider, while making available to me two of their good senior horses, Shoeman and Beefeater. The plan was that I try to qualify for the Canadian equestrian team going to the Munich Olympics. We were thrilled with this opportunity. Every weekend Lynn and I would drive to the Cudney farm at Winona, in the Ontario fruit belt around Niagara Falls. It was a long drive, but at least someone else was now helping with the horse bills.

We went on the 1971 fall international circuit, which then consisted of Harrisburg in Pennsylvania, Washington, D.C., New York, and the Royal Winter Fair in Toronto. I was *not* a star. I know now I was trying too hard. Wanting the horse to perform better, I departed from the basics that got me on the team in the first place. A horse cannot know that this is his rider's first time on the Canadian equestrian team: a creature of habit, he only knows that his partner has changed in some fundamental way.

My first tour with the Canadian team, then, went badly. Since I did not qualify for the team at the Royal Winter Fair, it was decided that I would ride there in the Open Jumper Division. This is a separate division, with some classes combined to include both national and international riders. Same jumps, just down a notch in terms of prestige and prize money. With War Machine at the Royal I won five classes and was Open Jumper Champion; with Shoeman I won another class. Why could I not have done that in Washington or New York or Harrisburg? Because as soon as I was dropped from the team, I felt that the pressure was off. Over the years I have watched young riders – top-of-the-line riders – go through that same period of adjustment when they first ride for their national teams. They try too hard.

When you put on that red coat with your flag on it, you ride for Canada, and that is a *big* deal. I remember the first time I won an international class: I was out in the ring, and looking up at the flag while they played "O Canada". It brought tears to my eyes. Special then, it is still special today. There is nothing like it. Winning a big cheque in a competition is thrilling too, but in a very different way. I know of no rider in the world who will not ride as hard or harder to win a class for his or her country as for the big money. I am proud of that element in the sport.

I did qualify for the 1972 Olympics. However, just before going, War Machine got hurt, so as a result I took Shoeman and Beefeater to Munich, where I was the reserve rider for both the three-day event team — dressage, cross-country, and stadium jumping combined — and the show jumping team. When one of the show-jumping riders, Barbara Simpson Kerr, dropped out because of an injury to one of her horses, I took her place in the Nations' Cup competition in show jumping, riding Shoeman. I could not have asked for a better Olympic partner than Shoeman. He was brave, experienced, and a competent show jumper.

I was twenty-five years old, and it was the biggest course I had ever seen. My team-mates, Jimmy Elder, Jimmy Day, and Torchy Millar, were all a great help to me. (Torchy is no relation of mine, but we have grown weary of explaining that; lately, as a joke, we tell people that we *are* brothers.) Torchy had, and still has, a truly unusual gift for choosing a talented horse, and subsequently developing that jumping talent to its fullest potential. From Jimmy Elder I learned the meaning of the word "champion". We placed sixth in the Nations' Cup, and it was in itself an extraordinary experience. But this was Munich in 1972, and so I remember my first Olympic competition as a brutal one.

We were living in row housing in the Olympic village. The routine saw us out at 6:00 A.M. to catch the first bus to the barn. One day we came out and saw someone kneeling behind a bush with a gun in his hand, looking at an adjacent building. Suddenly he and several other gunmen — none in uniform — started waving us back. We looked over to where the Israelis were housed, and a man was standing there with a machine gun looking out the window at us. The hostage-taking was under way.

Shaken by this, we nevertheless went off to do our riding while the situation continued throughout that day. Later we watched as the Israeli athletes were all led out, each tied by the hands to the person in front, and put on a bus. Finally, news came of the massacre at the airport. I tried to understand what differences can cause people to do these things to each other. It made no sense then and makes no sense now.

Torchy Millar, veteran Canadian grand prix rider and trainer

Ian and I grew up in the Ottawa area. I've known him well since the early sixties. What's unusual about him is how motivated and focused he is: he sets an objective in his mind and is totally intent on achieving that objective.

He wants to win; wants it more than most. Another thing: he has an ability to learn from past mistakes, analyse them, categorize the information, file it away, and remember it.

His riding style is unusual in that it's so orthodox. He has a wonderful sense of rhythm and pace in a horse. His is better than anyone's, and he uses it very well. Ian likes to find a horse's natural balance, and then work off that.

He's an outstanding horseman. He doesn't rely on gimmickry, more on the fundamentals of horsemanship, like repetition. He teaches the horse in small increments, working around the horse's character. A lot of riders want to do that, but get distracted along the way. You only have to forget what you're doing for a day to undo three months' good work with a horse. Ian just stays with it. That focus he brings to a show he has at home as well.

I said that Ian can relate to a horse's character: Brother Sam was one of his earlier mounts. Ian made the horse work for him just by letting the horse do what he did best in the most comfortable way. That sounds easy, but it's not. Several good riders had Brother Sam, and they couldn't make it work. Ian just worked with the horse's idiosyncracies and built upon his strengths and tried to work around his weaknesses.

Ian embodies all the abilities combined in one package: the ability to ride, train a horse, and run a business. It's natural ability married with all these other things that have put Ian on top.

But in Canada, where such tragedies seem less likely, politics and sport continue to mix. I want to ride against the best in the world, and I do not want the best kept away because our government is having a fight with their government. At the Loblaws Classic in Toronto in 1989 there was wrangling over the work permit of a South African-born rider named Philip Smith; permission for him to compete was granted only at the very last minute. At the next show he was stopped. (As of the time of writing, he has landed immigrant status and is eligible to compete in Canada.) He is a wonderful rider, and I wanted him in the Classic so I could get a crack at him. I did not want to win because of his absence. Was it correct to bar him from the competition because of what we deem crimes or social inequities in his country? I do not hold with the argument that letting a South African ride in Canada means we condone apartheid. Because we play hockey against Russia, does that mean we condone Communism? I can see economic sanctions accomplishing something, but that is different. To ban a rider from competing because of his country's politics is a symbolic gesture, and in the real world, symbolic gestures count for little. What does the government of South Africa care that Philip Smith is barred from competing in Canada?

After the 1972 Olympics, Doug Cudney wanted Lynn and me to live on his farm and to have me ride for him. I told him that, while I appreciated the offer, we had set down roots. We had bought a broken-down farm we called Millar Brooke, just outside Perth, home base to a highly leveraged real-estate empire that my friend John Rivington and I were amassing. And besides, at that time there was no future – certainly no career – in being a rider. You would start as a rider and finish on the end of a pitchfork. I kept thinking of what John Woods had told me: "Make your money in business, and then have your horses the way you *want* to have your horses." I have always been an optimist at heart; I really believed that after Munich we would receive some financial backing and succeed in Perth, one way or another. I believed then and believe now that if you work long and hard enough, if you want it badly enough, the plan – whatever the plan – will come to fruition.

Today, I look back on the twists and turns in my career and I see miraculous good luck. For Nancy Woods and Lynn and me to buy War Machine and then to make the Canadian equestrian team: that was one miracle. To have Doug Cudney, simply because he liked me and wanted to help me, buy my horse and then essentially give the horse back to me, along with two other quality horses: that was more good fortune. After the Olympics, my decision to turn down his offer of work represented another piece of luck, because later Doug's business troubles prevented him from continuing with the horses. But the best luck of all was about to drop in my lap, just when the outlook seemed bleak.

One day in 1973, when our financial fortunes were looking particularly grim, the phone rang. On the phone was a woman named Jackie Morold. My life was about to take another intriguing turn.

"I need a rider," she said. "I want to develop a group of top show horses in this country, and I need somebody to do it with. Would you come and see me? I'm half an hour away."

Jackie Morold with one of Dwyer Hill Farms's champion hunters, Another Brother
(J. J. Walsh)

She was that kind of woman. When she decided to do something, she did it. Jackie Morold, I soon learned, was a Coors beer heiress. She was then in her mid-thirties and gifted, in the sense that she could play the guitar and piano and sing and write poetry, but she was also extremely sensitive. She had a tremendous gift when it came to communicating with horses.

Out of the blue had come a terrific opportunity. After we talked, I was given a ten-year contract and, in cooperation with trainer Randy Roy – a very astute horseman – I was taken on as the rider at Dwyer Hill Farms, not half an hour from our own farm in Perth. Randy could think like a horse better than anyone I had ever met. He could give me the horse's side of the conversation, and through my riding I responded.

An added bonus from this time was the opportunity to learn from George Morris. A show-jumping legend, known for his analytical genius and flair for instruction, he just happened to have been a childhood friend of Jackie Morold.

When Jackie had told George that she was considering me as her resident rider at Dwyer Hill, he had advised against it. He felt then that I was "a crude rider". Jim Elder talked George into changing his mind, and George now concedes that he was wrong. I thus got the job and, as a pupil of the sport, my luck in finding the best instructors continued. On numerous occasions I would join Randy (who had already trained with George in barn management) at George's farm in Pittstown, New Jersey, for week-long schooling sessions. George gave me the polish I needed. He organized all my knowledge and skills into a system, putting a label on everything, introducing me to terminology I did not possess. George Morris took the mystique out of learning to ride. I learned a great deal just by watching him teach, and over time I took his ideas on horse gymnastics and expanded on them.

With Randy Roy (left) at
Dwyer Hill Farms

Now Lynn operated a riding school and a breeding program at Millar Brooke while I drove off to work at Dwyer Hill and continued to pursue my business interests. Eventually, Dwyer Hill Farms would win all over North America: it was a class outfit and quickly established itself as a formidable stable.

There was only one fly in the ointment: Dwyer Hill Farms was a single-owner operation. In these situations, the owner comes to expect, and the rider may be tempted to deliver, total and unequivocal devotion to the cause — at the expense of everything else. The rider's life and that of the owner become intertwined. At Dwyer Hill, the commitment required of Jackie, Randy, and myself was total and continued twenty-four hours a day. I dined with Jackie and her husband, Karl; I saw them socially, evenings and on weekends. Such a personal relationship offered both advantages and disadvantages. The rider in a one-owner operation may have a rewarding experience because of goals he shares with the owner; on the other hand, the rider's life is very much controlled and influenced by that owner's opinions and feelings. The result is a certain loss of independence, and even a certain vulnerability.

Karl Morold suggested constantly that Lynn and I sell our farm at Perth and move to Dwyer Hill, where he would build us a house. Lynn and I resisted; we felt it was important for us to develop Millar Brooke Farm, which we had owned for a year and a half before I began to ride with Dwyer Hill. In the end, keeping Millar Brooke turned out to be a wise move.

Randy Roy, trainer, Hunters Glen, King, Ontario

Ian and I were at Dwyer Hill, near Ottawa: me as trainer and him as rider. Early on I contemplated going back to school, and he took me aside — he's so brilliant — and said that there was a tremendous opportunity here. He had a vision. He saw that this was an avenue for a career, that he had a lot to learn from me, and together we could do it. He said we could complement each other.

I'll never forget the first day at Dwyer Hill. Ian said, "Randy, I want you to teach me how to ride a hunter." And I thought, Ian's been to the Olympics and he's asking me to teach him how to ride a hunter! So I put him on this hunter I had trained called Jet Flight, and I gave him a flat lesson: how to make the hunter look smooth. And he did every single thing I said. He got himself out of the tack, he made himself look smaller — because he has that huge upper body.

That told me how badly he wanted success. He would do everything to attain it. I wanted it really badly too. That was the launching of an eight-year partnership. He was that rare combination: a rider successful both in the hunter ring and at the grand prix level in show jumping. He did it better than anyone. He took that form and style he had learned in the hunter ring to the show ring. It made Ian ride smoothly. Today he rides around the jumper course, and it looks like he's riding a hunter course.

We talked through everything. We had to. We were always at opposite ends of the pole. We would meet somewhere in the middle. If we couldn't, we didn't do it. Everything I did with him I had to absolutely convince him beyond a shadow of a doubt. It was the longest process, always a battle, but we both ended up with so much respect for each other. As tough and aggressive as Ian was, I was too. He could be intimidating, and I'm methodical, conservative. I'm long-term; he was short-term (now he's long-term). I had tunnel-vision; he was progressive. He's gotten so smart about everything.

No barn came on the map as fast as Dwyer Hill did. We were famous in no time at all. With the hunters and the jumpers, we were champion or reserve champion at every show.

Ian's very serious, totally serious, about the horse business. And yet he's so much fun, wild at a party. Great storyteller. He'd joke in the barn. He'd tease; he loves to get people going. He's dedicated, ambitious, has this freakish winning instinct. Freakish. It's like he's possessed. He's a born winner, and the hardest, poorest loser I've ever seen.

The most difficult thing was to get Ian to adjust to losing, and he's still not there. And he should never be. He once said, "Show me a good loser and I'll show you a loser." I'll never forget that. And he's right. He taught me some of that killer instinct. He later learned to channel it. But right after a loss I couldn't talk to him about it: I had to let him blow off. I learned timing with him, because he was so fiery. I could see then that he would be where he is today.

He was always so smart about the money. He taught me how to make money, where to put it. He gave me so much incentive. If I'm well off today, I owe him everything for that.

Two of his secrets in the ring are his lower leg position and strength and the incredible accuracy of his eye. Ian, better than anyone, will gallop, fly blind, through an impossible turn to a jump and never ever think about looking for a distance "back when". It's all instinct. Ian lets his horse jump with a very round bascule, a very round back. He gives the horse a lot of freedom. There's never any impairment; he lets the horse show all his scope and talent. Horses put out for him, because he's a very generous rider in the air. He does it like nobody else.

We worked on training horses in form and style at Dwyer Hill, so that when Ian put them in one of these impossible situations I've just described, their instinct was to come out of it with their legs up and they'd miss the rails. We never schooled the horses to trap them; we schooled them to think they could do anything. I had a line: "Ian could ride a broom around the course." He could ride a bad horse and make him look good, and one thing we did at Dwyer Hill — because we had all this money — was to do it first-class, and only ride the best horses. Excellence became a habit.

Ian is good at getting a little bit of something from everybody, and then using the right things. It would always bother me that Ian talked to so many people about so many things. I thought he would get cluttered, but he has a great screening capacity, which I love. He would sift through all this and come up with a better solution than anybody.

Big Ben is so scopey, and yet it's so easy for him. What other horses fight to jump, he steps over. In those long gallops he can make up three and four strides and seconds. Ian and the horse are such a great combination. Often the horse loses his balance and some of his co-ordination at the canter, because he gets a little excited, but Ian is never disturbed by that. Doesn't throw him off at all. If there's a way to have Big Ben at the next Olympics, Ian will have him there. He really is the best rider in the world.

Dwyer Hill Farms

As a major shareholder in the Coors beer company, Jackie Morold regularly received sizeable dividend and interest income. This provided the capital to operate both the Dywer Hill horse farm and the Dwyer Hill beef farm. The latter prospered, mainly due to a genetic accident. The farm produced a Simmental bull by the name of Polaris, who was born without horns and who passed that worth-while trait on to his offspring. Bulls often hurt each other with their horns, and removing them adds expense and can occasionally result in sickness or death for a bull. Polaris, therefore, became a famous and much-sought-after sire.

The horse operation comprised three divisions: commercial, breeding, and show jumping. The commercial operation consisted of fifty-five stalls for boarders and sale horses (bought specifically to be resold). The breeding operation included twenty stalls for sport horses; it was founded on a pair of German breeding horses that the Morolds had acquired in Europe. Later we added a thoroughbred stallion called Fair Swap, and, later still, the division produced thoroughbred race horses. The show division comprised twelve stalls, and that is where Randy and I spent most of our time developing, training, and maintaining the show string. We also had a hand in the other divisions, especially when new managers were hired.

We had some fine horses at Dwyer Hill: I went on the fall circuit with a get-started grand prix horse called Night Cat. Then came one called Countdown, a thoroughbred from the racetrack, where he had not exactly excelled. Someone once said of him that "as a racehorse he couldn't outrun a fat man in rubber boots." But Countdown was tough enough and a good horse. He took me to the Montreal Olympics in 1976 and to the Pan-American Games. I won my first grand prix in the United States, and quite a few Canadian grand prix with him. Eventually Brother Sam became the big horse, backed up by Countdown and by Bandit, a speed horse. With Brother Sam, I won my first international grand prix at the Royal Winter Fair; we also won an individual bronze and a team silver at the Pan-American Games in Puerto Rico in 1979. Then Brother Sam

Brother Sam competing as a hunter, before becoming a Grand Prix jumper. Here he jumps an oxer, or spread fence.
(Bob Foster)

was sold and Bandit was moved up to the grand prix ranks, where he shone.

We also had a small mare called Springer — a liberated mare. She always wanted to discuss things and did not take direction well on course. She won often, but she should have won more. She went on to become a notable junior jumper. The young girl who rode her later simply allowed the horse to make more decisions than I did; on grand prix courses the successful rider has to take greater charge, and the rider's mount has to accept that.

During my Dwyer Hill phase I continued to learn more and more about the sport's practical aspects, such as how to drive the tractor-trailers used to haul horses long distances. On one occasion Karl ordered a new diesel tractor with a thirteen-speed transmission and asked me to pick it up in Ottawa. I took thirty minutes just to start the thing — and only after reading the manual. Off I went. God must indeed look after fools.

When Karl ordered a new horse trailer, he and I went to Virginia to pick it up and drive it back to Dwyer Hill. We believed we were experienced truckers now. But as I was driving through Dwyer Hill's front gate with the brand new trailer, I put a hole the size of a football in its side. I was mortified; Karl was understanding. However, later this meant that after a stopover in North Carolina, when we were taking the horses to compete in Florida, I had to take the tractor-trailer overnight to Virginia to get it fixed. I had to be there at 7:00 A.M. It was one of the longest nights of my life: the trucks behind me on the two-lane highway over the mountains sat on their horns and urged me to go at their speed — or get off the road. Learning to operate and drive these rigs was just one more aspect of being a horseman. I had to learn on the job and in a hurry.

One of the International Horse Transport horse vans today
(Jayne Huddleston)

You have to have your own trucks in this sport — especially if you live a long way from competition sites, as we do. Four years ago, I formed a company called International Horse Transport with Claude Bollinger and a Kingston businessman named Gerry Bisaillon. Claude is the son of the aforementioned Fritz and Lilian Bollinger, longtime friends and business associates. Claude is a good trucker and a good horseman, a valuable combination when it comes to moving horses. Horses are vulnerable when they are on a trailer. That is one reason Claude always keeps someone with the horses to monitor them during the long haul. Ventilation is crucial: if they get too hot they can sweat and develop lung problems. A rough ride will consume a lot of the horses' energy; loading and unloading is also tricky and the occasion of many horse injuries. For all those reasons I formed this company. The transportation of horses is a critical, fragile piece of work.

One day in 1974 we were in Florida at a show. Lynn was some distance away, working with a horse, and Randy Roy, smiling, asked me if I had noticed something different about her.

"No," I said.

"Can't you see? Lynn is pregnant."

I stared at him in amazement.

"Just look at her," he said. She was standing sideways to us, and I could indeed see the beginnings of that unmistakeable little bulge in her profile.

"You're right!" I exclaimed. "She *is* pregnant."

I went to Lynn and asked her if there was something she had been meaning to tell me.

"Like what?"

"Are you pregnant?"

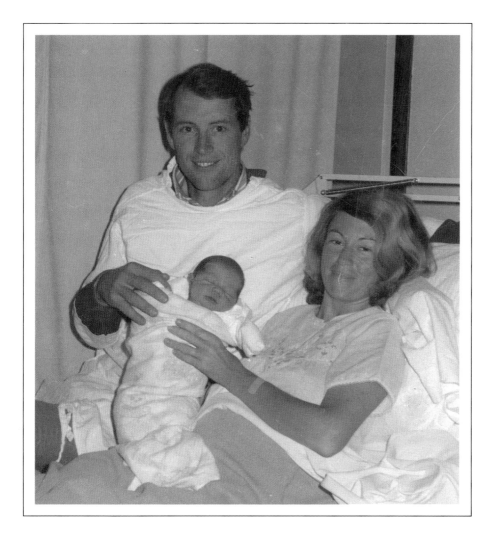

*Lynn and I at the hospital
just after Jonathon's birth*

"Yes," she said, and smiled. We had discussed having children, and though I had maintained my opposition, Lynn knew my mind better than I did. Relying on her wisdom and intuition, she took the decision herself, knowing I would see the light. And of course I did. We have always had that kind of partnership, one based on an intuitive and absolute understanding of each other.

As soon as she told me, I knew it was the right thing. It was like giving and getting at the same time the best possible Christmas present.

I remember my father saying once when I was a boy, "I thought I'd seen it all until I'd seen my newborn son at the hospital." Despite enduring a war, and despite his life experience to that point, nothing had prepared him for the sight of his own son. Only when I first saw Jonathon did I finally understand what he meant. What a moving and miraculous experience to see your own newborn child. Two years later Amy, our second miracle, was born. We went on the road with them, even when they were infants. Jonathon we put in a little wicker basket that could be carried like a hamper. If we went to dinner in a restaurant, we would ask for a corner table, and he would sleep all the way through the meal.

With Randy Roy (far left), Lynn and Jonathon (left rear), and the Dwyer Hill Farms staff at a Florida horse show. Cathy, Randy Roy's wife, is behind me, and to her left are Debbie Adams and Pat Moylen.

In the winter of 1980, the Dwyer Hill era came to a sudden and distressing end. Jackie and Karl came down to Florida — we were on the winter circuit as usual — and we were all sitting under the canopy of their camper for a barbeque. They told us that they were shutting down the jumper division and that we were to sell everything — horses, equipment — and let staff go. Right away. The announcement affected us deeply. We felt the shock that a family torn apart by divorce must feel. It was especially hard to break this news to staff when they were on the road. However, I should have seen it coming. During four years at Dwyer Hill, Brother Sam had won repeatedly. We would get offers all the time for him, offers of up to $250,000 for a horse we had bought for less than a fifth of that amount. Part of my job was to pass on those offers to Karl and Jackie, who always declined. In the summer of 1979 they stopped declining; they became much more interested in horse racing. The writing was on the wall and I did not see it.

Lynn and I were truly on our own once again. We were Millar Brooke Farm now, not Dwyer Hill. At horse shows we noticed a change in the way people approached us. If they were friendly before, now they were doubly so, and it occurred to us that we were no longer perceived as a threat. Our Dwyer Hill patrons had packed up and left. I did not like all this friendliness one bit; I had liked it better when people were friendly to our faces but talking behind our backs and wishing we would fall on our ears. When that Dwyer Hill Farm van turned up at horse shows, people had just known that a certain percentage of the prize money and ribbons was gone.

The bad news was that Lynn and I had horses, but no first-stringers. The good news was that by 1980, we did have all the skills we needed to run a first-class horse operation. Lynn had always believed that as a rider I would be a late-bloomer, and she was right. I was thirty-three, and I had run up a score of grand prix victories after my first at the age of twenty-one. Lynn was a shrewd buyer and trainer. But would we, now on our own, get the horses we needed? When the shock of the Dwyer Hill demise had subsided, I had no doubt that we would rise to the challenge. George Morris and all my other teachers had, in effect, given me a university education in matters equine. I felt I was qualified, and as important, I felt I would be perceived that way. And I wanted to do it all with Lynn.

Solo flyers now, we worked hard. We would take thirty horses to a tournament and compete in both the jumper ring and the hunter ring. The hunter ring features lower jumps and has its roots in fox hunting. The judging is subjective and considers not the rider, but the horse's jumping style, his way of moving, and his training. There we were, battling for every class with ponies, children's hunters, junior hunters, amateur hunters, junior jumpers. Life was a zoo. I was driving up and down the road, three and four trips to the same show, all night long and all day long.

But as usual, luck shone on our enterprise.

Two things happened. First, the Texan who had bought Brother Sam from the Morolds had had no success using an American professional rider with the horse. One day in that hot summer of 1980, the Texan, a man named John K. Hoff, called with an offer.

"Here's what I'm going to do," he said. "I'm going to send you Brother Sam. I don't want to see any bills. I don't want to hear any bad news. If something good happens, you call me. If there is prize money over expenses, send it to me. I don't want to hear about bills and I don't want grief." I had Brother Sam back.

Second, from Dwyer Hill Farms I got Warrior, a half-brother to Brother Sam. Riding Warrior gave me a real sense of *déjà vu*, for he was so much like Brother Sam. I remember when we bought the four-year-old Warrior: Jackie Morold was sitting on the grass under a tree and watching me ride him. Afterwards, I looked at Jackie and she looked at me, and we shared the same thought. Riding Warrior was exactly like riding Brother Sam. Randy thought we had lost our minds. Warrior's qualities, in fact, weren't so apparent to the eye; nor could Randy fathom the *déjà vu* that both Jackie and I were sensing. But we bought the horse anyway, and he eventually became a wonderful grand prix entry.

When I had first joined Dwyer Hill, I had signed a two-way, long-term contract with the Morolds, a rather airtight one. It meant that a sizeable sum would come my way if the contract was broken short of the

Warrior jumping in Wolfs-burg, West Germany, 1986
(Jayne Huddleston)

designated period. Similarly, I would forfeit the same amount were I the one to break the contract. There was some hard negotiating between Karl and me over how this contract was to be settled, but in the end it was agreed that, as part of the settlement, Lynn and I would become half-owners of Warrior, along with Fritz and Lilian Bollinger.

With Warrior and Brother Sam, Lynn and I were back in the ribbons, once again a threat to competitors at horse shows. Their friendly smiles dissipated a little.

CHAPTER 5

Millar Brooke
Comes of Age

W hen Lynn and I had begun the hunt for an affordable farm back
in the early 1970s, we had looked at several wonderful places
near Ottawa, but they were beyond our means. Within our means,
more or less, was Charlie Bolton's broken-down old place southeast
of Perth. For $35,000, we bought five hundred acres bordering on
the Tay River. Lynn named it Millar Brooke, because a small creek
traversed the property. It was a long way from being the homestead
we imagined.

The cedar shingles on the house were falling off in great patches, and
the front porch sagged miserably. With the shingles gone, the rain had
come in, and, as Charlie grew older and the rain invaded a room, he had
simply moved his meagre belongings to the next room. By the time we
took possession, Charlie was down to his last dry room. There was a foot
and a half of water in the basement. Hay was growing right up to the
house. Seven outbuildings were by degrees heading for horizontal.

*The house at Millar
Brooke Farm, with the
swimming pool at right.
The stable and arena
complex are in the back-
ground at right, and the
veterinary clinic is in the
background at left.*
(Jayne Huddleston)

The main barn (through door at right) adjoins the arena, which extends to the additional barn straight ahead.
(Jayne Huddleston)

Today, visitors to Millar Brooke Farm drive up a half-mile-long dirt road from the highway that links the village of Rideau Ferry and the town of Perth. On the left as you drive up are the high white fences that horse owners tend to favour. Opposite the paddocks is Charlie Bolton's old house, looking much improved. The red-brick farmhouse has been accented by black shutters, a new roof keeps the rooms dry, and perhaps Charlie would have approved of the addition and the swimming pool. Further along the road beyond the house is a large L-shaped building. This is a barn with stables at each end of the L — containing twenty-five stalls altogether — and an indoor arena in the middle, allowing horses to enter the ring from either stable.

Facing the main entrance to the indoor ring is a sophisticated equine hospital, run under a lease arrangement with Dr. John Atack. He and his wife, Dr. Linda Berthiaume, live in quarters above the clinic. Behind the house and barn are outdoor jumping areas, one sandy, one grass-topped. If the whole operation seems neat and orderly, it is not because I have a fixation on neatness. It is because the neat and orderly way is almost always the most efficient way.

My standards are high, and I take few vacations. The ten grooms and stablehands at Millar Brooke have come to realize that their employer is a perfectionist. A former employee once told an Ottawa journalist, exaggerating a little, that "Ian treats everyone like a horse. If you don't work out, you're shot or sent to the glue factory." Others have remarked on the extraordinary loyalty of Millar Brooke staff. More recently, another journalist visiting Millar Brooke Farm asked head groom Sandi Patterson what it was like working for a perfectionist. "Maybe," she told him, "he's not the only perfectionist around here." I could have kissed her for saying that.

The front entrance of the barn and arena complex, with the equine hospital to the left
(Jayne Huddleston)

By 1980, Millar Brooke was beginning to look like it does today. The eighties would see the farm grow and achieve numerous individual honours, but that one prize — an Olympic gold medal — continues to elude us to this day. But not for lack of desire. I remember being at a horse show in 1968 when it was announced over the loudspeaker that the Canadian team had won a gold medal at the Mexico Olympics. We were all so proud. I remember thinking, "I can't wait to get on the team and do something like that." I believe I have another ten years or more of jumping left to me, so perhaps there will be more chances to mount that podium.

In 1980 I came as close as I ever have. That year I did earn a gold medal and it should have counted, because it was a team gold won competing against the major world powers in show jumping, and within the sport it was considered veritable Olympic gold. But this was the ersatz Olympics of 1980, and the victory would go in the record books with an asterisk beside it.

When the Soviets invaded Afghanistan that year, and the western world responded by boycotting the Moscow Olympics, alternate Olympics for show jumping were held in Rotterdam. Should the Canadians send a team? A group of us were pondering that question one day in Bromont, Quebec, under the canopy of the Millar Brooke camper trailer. All the eligible riders for such a team were there, along with the chairman of the team and the *chef d'équipe*.

Finally, I said, "You know, there's one little problem in not going."
Someone asked, "What's that?"
"I've never won a competition in my life that I didn't enter."
Granted, the odds against this particular team winning were long. But it was the right team, made up of four seasoned veterans. There were

Jimmy Elder, Mark Laskin, Michel Vaillancourt, and myself. Although we were a little short in the quality of our horses, we were long on savvy, toughness, and determination. At the time, I was riding Brother Sam, that talented, capable horse whose greatness came from his heart. If Olympic victory could be coaxed out of Brother Sam and these other horses, we four were the ones to do it.

The decision was taken. We were going. All the great show-jumping nations were sending teams too, but they decided to prepare for Rotterdam by first going to shows in Aachen, Germany, and Hickstead, England. Tom Gayford, a team gold medalist at the 1968 Olympics and now our *chef d'équipe*, made a shrewd move. Smart about peaking horses and riders, he decided that the Canadian team would go to a small international show in Dinard, France, while the big guns were jumping mountains with their fabulous horses at Aachen and Hickstead. We won a great deal at Dinard, and we left thinking we were superstars.

The format at Rotterdam went like this: a "welcome" class; then the Nations' Cup, two rounds over a big course; and finally the individual competition, which got very tough. The Canadian riders cruised around the welcome class, riding easily and confidently. Then came the Nations'

Jim Elder, team gold medallist for Canada at the Mexico Olympics in 1968 and at the Rotterdam Alternate Olympics in 1980

When I first saw Ian, he was a long lanky kid, riding with arms and legs going all over the place. Riders are usually compact, so size was definitely against him. But he rode determinedly. His success stems from his desire, and from watching a lot of people. An exceptional trainer, he's very good at preparing his horses.

When we were riding together, it was really a weekend sport. He decided he was going to make a career out of it. It could have been a long time between paycheques. He took a big gamble, and he rides that way. But he covers his options well. He has back-up horses, as all the top riders have. He's also a hard worker and very analytical.

The top riders, like Ian, are strong individuals. You have to push hard. Sometimes you have to beat your friends in the ring. You have to blank all that out. Ian's tough physically and mentally. In a sport with few superlatives, Ian's a superstar. And it's not just because of Big Ben. We've all seen Ian win on mediocre horses.

Cup, a long and arduous competition, involving twenty national teams and 144 individual rounds that took some ten hours to complete.

I remember I rode third on the team, and after finishing my two rounds — one with four faults, one clean — I sat down in the stands with Mark Laskin and Michel Vaillancourt, and I said, "So, how's it shaping up?"

One of them said, "Well, we're looking very good. Depending on what these last four or five riders do, we're going to get a medal."

Jimmy Elder had a good round, but not a score to improve our standing. There were several top-of-the-line riders to go, so each would have to take down one or two rails for us to be successful. Still to ride were Hugo Simon of Austria on Gladstone, John Whitaker of Great Britain on Ryan's Son, and Gerd Wiltfang of West Germany, then World Champion, on Roman. All these famous horse-rider combinations had to collect some faults — and they did. First, the Canadian team was going to be fourth, then we were in line for the bronze, then the silver medal loomed, and finally the gold was in our grasp. The course was extremely tough, and all these nations had sent their strongest combinations last.

To emerge victorious on a day like this was incredible. We were like the little engine going up the side of the mountain. We-thought-we-could. We-thought-we-could. We-thought-we-could.

But in this story the mountain eventually got too steep for the little engine: in the individual competition none of us finished better than fifteenth. Never mind. We had the team gold, and we were thrilled. When we came back to Canada, we appeared on the CBC-TV program *Front Page Challenge*, the longest-running show in Canadian television. The panel tries, by a series of questions, to guess the identity of newsmakers, who are hidden from their view. They guessed us in no time — and this when our sport had scant recognition in Canada.

In 1984, the Olympics were held in Los Angeles. My plan was to ride Warrior, to this point my most successful grand prix horse. He was a fine and sensitive horse who would brood in his stall for days if someone was harsh with him (and take a long time to forgive the transgressor). Warrior had Brother Sam's heart and the same technical problem at the jumps (sometimes he didn't fold his front legs tightly and quickly enough); they were like clones. The only difference was that Brother Sam was long in the back, and Warrior was shorter, making the problem easier to deal with. Warrior and I connected very well. But when he pulled muscles in his back, Big Ben — then an inexperienced horse — was pressed into service. We fared passably well in the team competition, with Big Ben placing better than any other Canadian entry, and the Canadian team came in fourth. In 1988, in Seoul, Korea, Big Ben and I were to be very much a threat for a medal, and would just miss one in the Nations' Cup, as the Canadian team again came in fourth.

There will perhaps be other Olympics, and perhaps other medals. Meanwhile, Millar Brooke remains one of the most successful show-jumping operations in the world. The winning of back-to-back World Cups, in 1988 and 1989, stands as a rare achievement. Good luck and hard work brought me to the senior ranks of a very competitive sport. Only continued hard work will keep me there.

A day at home begins at about 7:30 A.M. with the stretching exercises I have done every morning for the past eight years. My career was almost ended by back trouble, and the regimen I developed to keep it at bay is one I follow religiously. My father, uncle, and cousin all suffered back problems. My own back began to bother me when I was eighteen with severe and intermittent muscle spasms. In 1981, when I was thirty-four years old, there was a bleak period in my life when the pain would not abate.

That year we had brought about thirty horses to the Toronto Spring Show on the grounds of the Canadian National Exhibition. I was to ride twenty-four of them — a horrendous amount of work. I had also helped to unload a lot of heavy trunks. Later, while competing in a class, I was cantering to jump number three, when I felt an odd twinge. By the eighth and final jump, my back had gone into a severe spasm and I could walk later only with difficulty. Other riders were found to take over my work at the show. Doctors, though, could find nothing, and for the first (but not the last) time, I consulted a chiropractor, Dr. Tom Offen.

As I frequently do when confronted with a problem, I began to read about it and talk to people. I discovered that a friend was taking biotin, a vitamin supplement often fed to horses to promote growth and quality in their hooves and to chickens to make their beaks stronger. Lynn and I had noticed that horses on biotin had fewer back injuries. It occurred to me that what is good for the horse might be good for the rider; I started taking biotin. Later I talked to an American rider who also had back trouble. He reasoned that the rider's back is vulnerable because the muscles at the thigh become overly strong from riding and do not stretch, forcing muscles in the lower back to take on their work.

Looking for answers to my back problem, I shopped around among the experts: a back specialist in Ottawa, a doctor at the sports-injury clinic, a sports physiotherapist, as well as a physician with a background in herbal medicine, and the aforementioned chiropractor. Each one had slightly different, even conflicting, advice. By sifting through what each had told me, and by reading books and articles, I devised a program for managing my back.

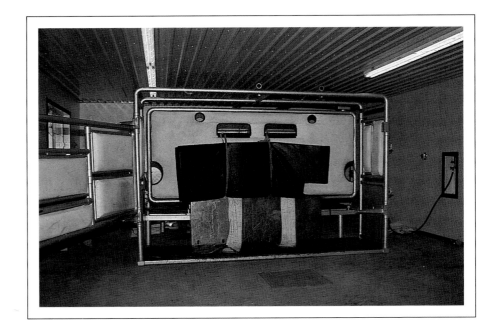

The operating table in the equine hospital. Here, the table is upright, ready for a horse to be positioned, after which the table would be altered to the horizontal for surgery.
(Jayne Huddleston)

I began doing a series of daily exercises that stretch my lower back and upper legs. Part of the ritual is twenty-five to thirty sit-ups to keep a little tone in the abdomen, the theory being that the stronger the abdomen, the more work it will take from the back. All this is combined with regular maintenance visits to my good friend and chiropractor, Dr. Offen. I began this program in 1982, and I have had no problems since. I like to draw lessons from experience. The lesson here was the wisdom of considering a wide range of expert medical advice before deciding on my own what course to follow. The lesson holds just as true in managing the health of our horses. Vets, blacksmiths, and horse chiropractors all have ideas; my task is to assemble their suggestions and decide on the most appropriate course of action.

My breakfast is usually raisin bran and bananas, or sometimes just fruit. Doctors generally give it little credence, but I do subscribe to certain aspects of the Fit for Life diet, which argues that between 5:00 A.M. and 12:00 P.M. the body is in a cleansing mode and that fruit alone best suits that purpose. I like fruit anyway. At horse shows I can sometimes be seen eating an apple while walking the course. But the apple is also meant to fend off hypoglycemia. My low blood sugar has gotten me into trouble on several occasions; at high-pressure competitions you are keyed up and you burn off more energy than normal. While competing in the ring in Cleveland ten years ago, and in Tampa one year ago, I found myself suddenly going blank and off course. I had no idea what city I was in, let alone which jump was next. I did regain my composure, but I have made a habit since of eating fruit when there is no time during the competition for a good meal. Multiple vitamins — especially vitamin E — are also part of my daily routine.

Inside the arena
(Jayne Huddleston)

My constitution, perhaps aided by my diet, is such that I am almost never sick. I consider myself fortunate in that regard.

By 9:00 A.M. I am either in the Millar Brooke arena or in one of the outdoor jumping areas, riding and training horses. I like to spend a minimum of forty-five minutes with each horse, and I make a point of riding Big Ben every day. The riding of younger horses is something I share with our current resident rider. The horses are brought into the arena according to a schedule Lynn and I have drawn up the night before, or maybe three or four days before if we are working towards a particular show. The schedule is posted in the barn for grooms, along with particular instructions on tack. Some days there is time for lunch, some days not. I often ride until three or four in the afternoon.

During much of this training, and during many competitions, Lynn is there with her advice and input. She is my wife, my partner, and my eyes on the ground, spotting things that I can't see from the saddle. She is also a shrewd horsewoman in her own right. Another horsewoman, our good friend Faith Berghuis of Brockville, Ontario, once called her "the Rock of Gibraltar, the power behind the throne". That barely begins to describe how important she has been to the success of our operation. Only recently, with the hiring of others to take on some of her responsibilities, has Lynn's workload diminished.

Late in the afternoon, when the riding and training are finished for that day, I climb the stairs in the arena and go to my office. Its walls are of rough pine, and most of the blank space is occupied by ribbons, framed awards, and — before someone removed them in the interests of tidiness — phrases I had gathered here and there. One I liked was "I'd rather buy a good horse from a bad man than a bad horse from a good man." The kernel of wisdom in this saying is perhaps obvious, but sometimes forgotten: the horse's character matters, not the seller's.

My desk in the office. A window in the opposite wall overlooks the indoor arena.
(Jayne Huddleston)

I seem to want to collect such sayings, parables, metaphors. Some people who know me believe that my habit comes from teaching horses all my life. My instinct is always to simplify, to make things run more efficiently. Perhaps that is true, and the parables point me in the direction of efficiency.

Music is usually playing from a sound system that feeds both into the arena and into my office. I love music — the Eagles, Eric Clapton, Rod Stewart, Dire Straits, the Beatles — and I really notice when it is *not* on.

All day my assistant, Paula Heinemann, has been fielding calls and ranking them in order of importance. Occasionally I can be seen riding around the ring with the portable phone glued to one ear; some calls — from overseas, for example — will not wait. The phone is an instrument of torture at Millar Brooke, but for me the only thing worse than a constantly ringing phone is one that does not ring at all. There is, you see, no pleasing me.

Someone once said, after watching me for a day at Millar Brooke, that I was like a general gathering reports from various battlefronts. A typical day, built around the normal duties of riding and training, can cover a lot of territory. Neither in mind nor body do I stay still very long.

I might be heard on the phone to John Rivington, my business partner: "How's that land deal in Perth coming along? Meet you at six in Smiths Falls?"

Then in the barn, talking to Glen Bishop, the farm manager: "Have you got all the hay off the north field yet? Was the tractor still making that weird noise?"

Then outside to a bulldozer-operator called in to rework one of the outdoor jumping areas: "That low area over there; can you fill that in? Maybe redirect the drainage so it's moving towards the tree line?"

A rare moment of relaxation when the children were younger.

Then in the arena to Sandi: "Did you remember to pack an extra saddle for Jonathon for that show in Collingwood next week?"

Then to Paula: "How's our breeding program with El Futuro? Was that semen shipped on time?"

Then to Lynn: "Are we still going on Friday to Fort Erie to look at those track horses?" On and on. . .

Evenings are spent on horse and other business: entry forms for shows have to be filled in, there are evening meetings with sponsors and business partners, I sit on equestrian committees, I help organize a new show that is being developed in Ottawa. Supper is a hit-or-miss affair. Small wonder that I watch almost no television, and, unlike many other riders, follow no other sports. Sometimes there is time in an evening at home for the family to watch a rented video. Lynn prefers films with happy endings; I like films with action. What we both want is a diversion from the world of show jumping.

Amid all this frenzy there is always time to laugh. I usually have jokes to tell, mostly bad ones, and no one appreciates them more than I do. Truly, I am my own best audience. My humour gives me away: if I tease someone, it is because I like them (I tease, Lynn, for example, constantly), and if I turn sarcastic, my humour has become an outlet for my anger.

I am convinced that we all have an optimum stress level. Somewhere on the scale of stress between total relaxation and racing on ten cups of coffee is where I function best, but my preferred place is decidedly closer to the top end. If stress puts me past that level, however, I use a yoga technique: I imagine that part of my body where the tension is gathering, where my neck meets my shoulders, for example. Then I focus on my right hand and work my way back, gradually forming a wave of relaxation. If I encounter resistance, I stop and start over just before the point of tension. This technique was originally taught to me as a sleeping exercise, but sometimes I will quietly do it while sitting at a

(Above) Amy and Jonathon have grown up on the road. Here they help by cleaning tack trunks.

(Left) Amy (with trophy) and Jonathon on their ponies at the Perth Fair about 1984.
(*Smith Falls Record* News Photo)

horse show. The more you practise this self-preservation skill, the more adept you become.

Lynn, Jonathon, and Amy have grown used to the pace of my life. They are neither intimidated by it nor much bothered by it. The hectic nature of my life is a given. If I am on the phone in my office and she's home, Amy might simply wander in and make herself comfortable on the wicker couch facing my oak desk. When I am free, she will tell me how her own riding is going, launch the idea of pizza for lunch, maybe argue the case for the family all going to the cottage for the night.

A few years ago we bought a little cottage about a twenty-minute drive from our home. Lynn pushed strongly for this haven. Jonathon and Amy are always pressing us to take them there in the summer. The lake is quiet; they can putter in the canoe or water-ski behind the small power-boat. Best of all, there is no phone.

Sometimes I wonder if my children are going to wake up one day and question why their father is a maniac, dragging them to horse shows, working all the time. At some point they will have to decide if this is the all-consuming life they want to lead.

Jonathon, who is fifteen at the time of writing, has great natural riding talent, a nice feel for horses, and an uncanny ability to calm a troubled horse. Horses automatically like Jonathon. He is relaxed and patient, even permissive, with them. Not so long ago a friend of ours, Frances O'Brien, was at an outdoor show and saw what she thought

Our home away from home. The house trailer that we live in at many horse shows in North America.
(Jayne Huddleston)

was me riding some distance away, although she did not recognize the horse. But no, it was Jonathon. That is how similar our riding styles are. Still, his interest peaks and wanes.

Amy, on the other hand, is by nature a more demanding rider. Her interest at this point is stronger and she spends more time with the horses. She is also well-liked by the horses, but she always wants to teach and train them. She is thirteen, she wants a lot done, and right away. Hers is an equal but different talent.

Both are gifted riders, but, in the long run, attitude in a rider is as important as aptitude. Not everyone has what it takes to be on the road thirty-six weeks of the year.

If days at home are mostly frantic, years are as well. January is devoted to heavy training and small schooling shows around Canton, New York. February sees us back at Millar Brooke, and during the second week we go either to Arizona or Florida to begin the winter circuit with ten or twelve horses. In 1989, our first show was in Venice, Florida. Through March and April we were mostly in Tampa for big shows, culminating in the World Cup Final. By late April, the Ontario circuit had begun, and by mid-November we had been to Edmonton, Calgary, Bromont in Quebec, Cincinnati, Ottawa, Collingwood in Ontario, back to Calgary, Halifax, Stuttgart, New York, Toronto, Bordeaux, Brussels, and more. Thirty-six weeks on the highway, in airplanes and airports, sleeping in hotels. On the road in North America, home is often our trailer, which we park in the "camper cities" that form at country shows. The trailer is long and roomy, with ample space to sleep the four of us, a good stereo system, a shower and adequate kitchen, even a small washer and dryer.

Chasing ribbons. Riding and training horses. Teaching riders. That has been my life for more than two decades, and even were I to win the lottery, there is little I would change. I love what I do, and not many can say that. I am absorbed by it. I cannot imagine a life without horses. There are always new horses on the horizon, with new personalities, new

The laneway that joins the highway and Millar Brooke Farm. I am on Brother Sam (left) and one of my students, Leonard MacCormack, is on Year of the Cat (right).

strengths, new possibilities. I love to win, but at least half my satisfaction comes from training and developing those horses. To purchase a grand prix horse is a great privilege, but to have a hand in the moulding of that talent offers even greater rewards.

I even love the smells associated with horses. Anyone who has worked around horses knows them: the leather of reins and saddle, the wood shavings put in stalls as bedding, the oil used in show rings to keep the dust down, the smell of a horse after a strong workout, the green fragrance of hay.

When I was a stockbroker I learned to do up to three things at once; talk on two phones while watching ticker tape, for instance. Today in my office I can still talk to someone, watch a horse out in the ring through the window, and have one ear tuned to the calls coming in to Paula. At horse shows, it is again convenient to parcel my attention: I can be riding and training a horse, watching other riders, and listening to scores on the loudspeaker. Doing three things at once is a neat trick; neater still is absolute focus on one thing. I was tested several years ago by a sports psychologist, Peter Jensen at York University, who told me that, in my ability to focus, to blot out everything but the task at hand, I was in the ninety-ninth percentile of athletes he had tested. I suspect I was born with this natural ability, which experience has refined.

There is indeed method in the Millar madness. I sometimes liken it to an overdrive gear in a car. The car can be in high gear without overly taxing the engine. In show-jumping events, the days become long — four to six hard days in a row, with the most important money class at the end, on the Sunday. Physically and mentally, riders feel worn. My biggest opportunity to win might come when I am not at my freshest. What keeps me strong to the end? I have always felt that what keeps me up is more than an adrenalin rush. Perhaps the body will react to adrenalin, but the mind reacts to something else. It is what I call focus; words such as *concentration*, *direction*, *discipline*, come close to catching its essence. *Focus* is the art of gathering all one's faculties to perform the task of competing. That I suffer from cold or the flu, that I am exhausted, or have a big meeting coming up — none of that matters when I compete. My focus on winning is total.

Of course, such intensity is not always appropriate. When I start on a project, I am determined to finish it. Even when it appears hopeless, I will continue. To a fault. I am still learning that there is a time to step back, analyse where I am going, and stop when the percentages are against success. When I was younger, I would never stop. Increasingly now I analyse, look at my chances, then decide.

But as important as analysis is, instinct is more important still when it comes to the purchase, training, and riding of horses. What has given me consistency and longevity in the sport are those instincts coupled with learned analytical skills that reduce the risk of error. I have always been more instinctive than analytical. In horses and in business — even in walking a show-jumping course — I get my instinctive impressions first and then follow them up with analysis.

In 1989, the grand prix ribbons — placed on the bridles or breast plates of top horses in a ceremony following the class — piled up for Millar Brooke Farm. It was a fabulous year not just because of our unusually high number of grand prix wins, but because of the different horses involved.

The year started with the World Cup win in Florida on Big Ben. Then Domingo won the grand prix at the Toronto Spring Show held at the Eglinton Equestrian Centre. El Futuro won the Chrysler Derby at Spruce Meadows in Calgary and was Canadian National Champion. Winchester won the Loblaws Classic in Toronto. Big Ben won in Cheltenham, Ontario. Isis won in Blainville, Quebec, and both Big Ben and Lonesome Dove won at the Tournament of Champions in Newmarket, Ontario. Big Ben ended the year with a dramatic flourish, winning two of the three European grand prix competitions we entered, at Stuttgart and Bor-

deaux. In Brussels, I competed on Winchester in a class that was run like the world championship: the top four riders at the competition ride their own and the three other horses in sequence. I won, and Winchester was outstanding, offering each of his four riders clean rounds in this important and prestigious event. In 1989, Millar Brooke won a total of ten grand prix victories, better by one than our previous best year of 1987.

El Futuro winning the 1989 Canadian National Show Jumping Championships. El Futuro wears ear covers to keep insects out of his ears.
(Jayne Huddleston)

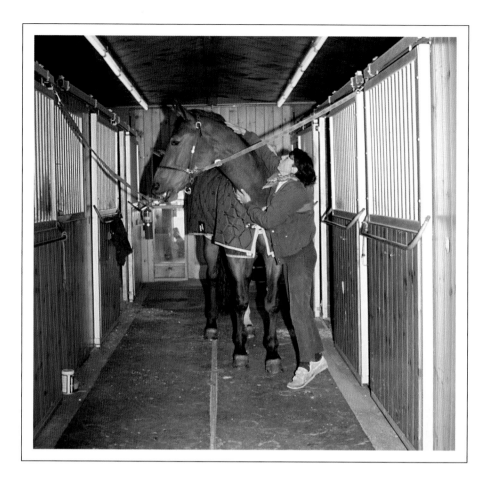

Groom Debbie Adams brushes Domingo in the aisle of the Millar Brooke barn.
(Jayne Huddleston)

There are several young horses in the Millar Brooke stable who could become very good indeed: Canadian Colours, Lonesome Dove, Domingo, and Future Vision, a seven-year-old gelding who has unusual power in his hind legs. He can kick that hind end and keep it there, as if he had a hinge in his back just behind the saddle. Put in human terms, imagine lying on your stomach and being able to raise your legs two or three feet off the ground. I am also hoping that a fine mare called Future Shock can come back from a serious tendon injury. And there is no reason why Big Ben, El Futuro, and Winchester cannot compete for years to come. Why should the future not be bright?

Before I retire I would like to have a hundred grand prix victories. At the time of writing, I have won seventy-four, including four or five jumping derbies. Although they are similar to grand prix courses, these are longer and feature some natural obstacles, such as steep banks, water jumps, and the devil's dyke.

As Millar Brooke has come of age, so has my standing in the sport. Over the years I have received some extraordinary fan mail from all over Canada and Europe. As show jumping has become more visible, its followers have become more interested in individual horses, and not just in riders' athletic endeavours but in their personal lives as well. One side of me finds the public attention a little tiring, at times superficial, occasionally even an invasion of my privacy. Another part of me, however, enjoys it.

I realize how important it is to show jumping that personalities in the sport relate to the public. Proud of my horses, of the Canadian equestrian team, and of my own accomplishments, I enjoy having all this recognized. I also realize that to many people, my life and Big Ben's life *do* mean something. We can have an influence, one hopes for the good, and that makes it all worth while.

I used to smoke the odd cigar, but only rarely at competitions if I thought young riders were present: I was concerned about a negative impact, especially since people tend to assign heroic qualities to certain athletes. People write to say that seeing Big Ben and me in a competition has quite literally changed their lives; they have been inspired in a way I barely understand. The reality is that I am just a human being with a God-given talent to ride a horse. I have worked hard at it, and I am supported by generous and loyal owners, a hard-working staff, and an understanding family. People create their own illusions, and sometimes they see me in ways I do not see myself at all. I have had to adjust to that fact.

This is the serious side of being a public figure. But by no means is it all serious. One regular correspondent to Millar Brooke is an eighty-eight-year-old woman from St. George, New Brunswick, who once began a letter, "Well, bless your old heart and buttons, as we say 'down east'...." Six horse-loving women who call themselves Cowgirls Inc. once wrote to express their support for the Canadian equestrian team. They gave their nicknames as Lefty, Big Red, Kissy, Deadeye, Babs, and Rosie. And much of the fan mail addressed to Millar Brooke Farm is not for me at all, but for a horse named Ben. Big Ben.

In 1987 a terminally ill teenager chose a ride on Big Ben as one of her last wishes.
(Jayne Huddleston)

CHAPTER 6

Big Ben: "Too Big, Too Ugly"

The mastery of a show-jumping course by horse and rider calls for grace and harmony and power. It can look easy, and to the untrained eye, the artistry is invisible. But show jumping, as every rider knows, can be humiliating. In a sport that ranks among the most dangerous, I too have a litany of scars, broken bones, and embarrassing falls, which I will relive later.

The point is, show jumping has many ways to keep riders humble. They do, for example, share the limelight. Someone watching a show-jumping event at the Royal Winter Fair in Toronto once asked a fellow spectator, who happened to be my wife, Lynn, "Help me with a name. Who's that guy who rides Big Ben?" Those who do not follow the sport may not know the name Ian Millar, but Big Ben they do know. Aficionados know the special qualities that make him great, along with his idiosyncrasies: he despises apples, for example, which most horses

On Big Ben in Wolfsburg, West Germany
(Jayne Huddleston)

Big Ben going over a wide water jump.
(Andy Rose)

love. Few horses in the history of the sport have achieved the recognition that Big Ben has. He is one of the best show-jumping horses in the world, and on certain days, unquestionably the best.

He stands 17.3 hands high, making him the largest successful grand prix horse in the world. (Big horses are not rare; big successful ones are). He has won more than one million dollars, a winning record unmatched in North America.

What else sets him apart — besides his contempt for apples? I have never encountered a horse with his phenomenal eyesight. Nor have I ever ridden a horse with such drive. If the trailer leaves Millar Brooke Farm without him, he whinnies and makes a terrible fuss. Big Ben is

unusually brave and aggressive for a gelding; he *really* loves to compete. Finally, there is his remarkable consistency. Two or three years at the top is all you can expect from horses competing at the grand prix level; Big Ben, in 1990 a mature fourteen years of age, is entering his seventh successful year of competition against the world's best horses.

How we found him and bought him is in one way typical of horse deals. You take a chance, you follow your instincts, you hope that luck is on your side. But the purchase of Big Ben, like the horse himself, was different. I have been as sure about only one other decision in my life, and that was to marry Lynn. From the moment I saw Big Ben, I knew what I would do.

It was late September 1983. I had been introduced to Emile Hendrix, a tall and solidly built rider on the Dutch national team. Emile has a rare talent: he knows the riding styles of different European and North American countries, what the riders need in a horse, and what a horse might fetch on either side of the Atlantic. He can mesh all that information and match horse and rider at the right price. A clever man, an ethical horseman, a brilliant culler of horses, he is one of the best horse dealers in the world.

We had been chatting at Spruce Meadows in Calgary about European horses, and when I told him that I was planning a trip to Brussels, he urged me to visit him while I was there, so when my business in Brussels was concluded, I did contact him. Emile told me about a certain horse in the Belgian countryside about an hour from Brussels, on the way to his home. I remember him saying, "You know, there's a horse. . . . I don't know whether you'd like him or not. He's a great big horse, and you've got to see him. You might really hate him, and it might be a total waste of time, but there's a chance you might find it interesting too." He was acting as agent for the seller, a Dutch rider named Bert Romp, but he wasn't selling hard.

Emile Hendrix, Dutch grand prix rider

Ian is gifted. He has the right character for show jumping: he gives 200 per cent to make something work, and even after all his results, he still concentrates like hell. He's deep into the details of the sport. Little things make him unique. He tries to control every little aspect that would cost him a ribbon. Away from the shows, you can have a wonderful time with Ian; but at the shows he's really concentrating.

Millar Brooke Farm was built up piece by piece, from nothing. Those things don't fall apart so fast. He worked hard to get the sponsors in Canada he has now. With his quality and results, he would have had an easier time of it in Europe — and especially England — where there is more media coverage of the sport.

I like him. We're close friends. We do a lot of horse business together, because the horse business is based on confidence. We try to do business in the long-term. Getting a chance to sell a horse to Ian is special.

He belongs among the best riders in the world. I think he has a beautiful family. For all kinds of reasons, he's an example for many riders.

We arrived at the farm, a professional-looking facility with an indoor arena still in the process of being built. A chestnut gelding was tied to a stall front. He had on a saddle, and a tall, ugly halter. We looked at him, and he looked at us — a little belligerently I thought. A tall, raw-boned horse, he was slim and had his head stuck up in the air. He failed to make a good first impression, but I liked his arrogance. There was an individual statement in his disposition.

I asked the other horsemen who were with us, "Anybody have an interest in buying this horse?" They said no. "Too big, too ugly," said one.

But there was something about this horse called Big Ben. He was being trained by Bert Romp, who has since become a rider for the Dutch team, but back then was just getting started. Bert had bought the horse in Belgium from his breeders, and many people knew about Big Ben. (It is unusual, though not rare, for Belgian horses to be given English names.) Henk Nooren, who for years has been one of the biggest and best dealers in Holland, and who is an excellent rider himself, had been to see the

*Big Ben as a four-year-old.
He was then known as
Winston.*

horse twice, and had plans to go back a third time. But he could not make
up his mind. Some interested buyers from Switzerland had looked at Big
Ben the day before we arrived on the scene, but they were just as
indecisive. All this was unusual. Normally, horse buyers decide in twenty
minutes or half an hour, but about Big Ben, none could decide.

The horse was seven years old by this time and still nobody was
buying him. Such a situation always makes me nervous. If my peers are
saying "no", then maybe I should listen to them — unless I have an ego
the size of a barn, which I do not. I have been put on the ground too
many times to have an ego like that. This sport, remember, is a humbling
one.

Everybody felt the same. They looked at this somewhat bad-
tempered horse, a big monster of a thing, not the best-looking, and what
they really saw was the proverbial bull in a china shop. He could jump,
but would he ever fit into today's indoor show rings, or handle the
courses? Could he be a modern-day show-jumper? If he was not too
clumsy, would he be able to shorten his stride? Given his size, would he
be fast enough? His blood line was also questionable: he was by a stallion
called Etretat, and there had been few proven horses by him. (Needless
to say, that stallion now commands greater interest.) And obviously if he
failed to work out, the downside was grim, because there could be no
other job for him. Selling him to a junior rider or riding him in the hunter
classes where the jumps are smaller were both out of the question. He
was a professional's horse, a top rider's horse. Or nothing.

I said, "Let's have a look at him." Bert mounted him and I watched Big Ben walk halfway down the side of the arena. Normally in a horse deal I sit back and let the seller present the horse to me. Not this time. I said, "Let me see him trot." And he trotted, again only halfway around the arena. I loved his trot. It was loose, easy, powerful. I said, "Let me see him canter." He picked up a canter, down one side of the arena. "Does he do a flying change?" I asked Bert. "Well, sort of," he replied. So Big Ben attempted the flying change, and though it was a little rough, he managed it.

All this had taken about two minutes. I walked over and made a little cross-pole jump about two feet high, and I said "Let me see him trot over this." He did. By this point I liked the horse a lot. "May I ride him?" I asked — again, an unusual request on my part. Normally I let the seller ride the horse for fifteen minutes on the flat; he may then jump him, put the jumps higher, and otherwise display the horse's talents. If I really liked what I saw, I might get on him myself. But for some reason I escalated the process this time. Everything was telling me, "I love this horse."

We put my saddle on him. European saddles are big and padded; in Canada we ride in a much flatter, less-padded saddle, which often will sit a little closer to the horse's withers. Big Ben was then a skinny horse whose withers protruded, as they still do. The saddle was on, but now his head was up in the air, his ears were back, and he was winding his tail — signs of displeasure. The minute I sat on him I sensed that something was bothering him. Wondering how the saddle fit, I put my finger under the front of it, only to find that it was too close to his withers. When I leaned forward the slightest bit, my weight pressed the front of the saddle downward onto the wither bone. Big Ben was *so* sensitive to this. Most horses, 99.9 per cent of horses, would have tolerated this discomfort. Not Big Ben.

I jumped off and found a pad to place under the saddle. When I got back on, he was a different horse. Here was a horse with a definite disposition. If he disliked something, I knew he was not going to keep quiet about it. I worked Big Ben a little on the flat, jumped some jumps. They had a whole course there, and I asked for certain jumps to be changed around. It took all of fifteen minutes. Ben's legs were correct and strong, sound, and unblemished. I liked the way he moved, his balance. I liked his technique, his instinct to jump, his power. And we immediately established a rapport.

Then, still on Big Ben, I motioned Emile to come over into a corner, and I said, "Look, obviously cut the best deal you can, — but buy this horse. For me. I want this horse." Emile took Bert aside, they shook hands, and we bought the horse — for $45,000.

With Big Ben (left) and Warrior in 1984
(Steve Forrester/*Perth Courier*)

Eve Mainwaring, a horse trainer and a long-time friend and supporter who lives in Brockville, not far from us, happened to be with me at the time. She was there to buy broodmares and younger horses. That night she said to me, "How are you going to pay for that horse?" I said, "I don't know." The normal procedure involves having veterinary work done in Europe, bringing the X-rays home, showing them to your own vet, doing blood tests; two or three weeks may pass before the buyer is obliged to send money. I believed I would find the money somehow. Eve had mixed feelings about the horse; he reminded her of another one that had not worked out, but she said, "You really like him, don't you?" I said, "I love him." And she bought half of him right there (Eve later bought a stallion called Fantast, a half-brother to Big Ben). Her feeling was that if I was that sure...

But we could have been wrong. What a modern horse has to do in the show ring is quite specific and complicated; knowledgeable horse people have in their minds the ideal sport horse. Big Ben's size alone would put him outside that preferred range. George Morris has said that, in show jumping today, horses sixteen to seventeen hands high are the ideal, and that any horse above or below that height is a freak.

I understood why potential buyers were cautious. Like many big horses, Big Ben had been slow to come along. As a young horse, I learned later, he had been notoriously skittish, slow to be broken and slow to learn (though once he learned something, he never forgot). Big Ben had also been hard to catch in the paddock, and by nature suspicious of people.

Bert Romp had owned the horse for only three months, but he was beginning to realize Big Ben's merits. Emile told me afterwards that Bert had wanted to raise the price during our dealing — not just as part of normal bargaining, but because he was becoming aware that he had a better horse than anyone imagined.

Emile also later told me an interesting story he had heard about Big Ben. Apparently, when the horse was only three years old, before he had even begun to be trained over jumps, his owner had turned him loose in a ring where jumps had been set up. A strange thing happened: Big Ben started to canter over the jumps, and he did that five times in a row. The owner had never seen a horse do that before. It was as if Big Ben was born with the desire to jump.

Looking back, I think our timing was impeccable. Had we been there a month or six weeks sooner we might not have seen Big Ben's good qualities, because Bert had only had him a short time and had only begun to train him. Had we been there a month later Big Ben almost certainly would have been gone. If not, he might have become prohibitively expensive, or Bert might have changed his mind about selling him at all. I took a chance, and my instincts paid off.

That night at Emile's, Eve confided to me she was troubled. Looking for a washroom in a back area of Bert's arena, she had come across a menacing-looking "tack rail". Normally these are jumping rails with tiny finishing nails one-eighth to one-quarter-inch long peppered into the wood. The idea is not to hurt the horse, but to make him feel a pinch every time he touches that rail with his feet. It is not a technique I approve of, but it is employed by some riders and trainers. Eve had never seen a tack rail like this. It looked like a medieval instrument of torture. The nails were huge and stuck out several inches. She was alarmed and called Emile over. I was out in the arena mounted on Big Ben while they were all huddled out of sight. They were disturbed, but by then the deal had been consummated.

The news concerned me as well. Was this awful thing once used on Big Ben to make him jump higher and more carefully and thus facilitate the sale? On the telephone, Emile described his concern to Bert, who had no idea what he was talking about. Finally, light dawned and Bert started to laugh. For a party at the arena some days before they had needed a coat rack, which they had fashioned by driving large nails into a rail and then hanging it between two standards. The "instrument of torture" was a coat rack. We all had a good chuckle over that, and I breathed easier.

Big Ben was born with the desire to jump.
(Andy Rose)

I was so excited about buying Big Ben that I called Lynn back home in Canada. We must have seen the film *E.T.* that year.

"Tell me about this horse," Lynn asked.

"I think the best way I can describe this horse," I said, referring to his looks, "is to say that his name should be E.T."

"Oh my God!" came the reply.

We brought him home with the three or four other horses we had bought, and they quarantined at Eve Mainwaring's farm, St. Alban's, before coming to Millar Brooke. While quarantined, they received their various flu shots and vaccinations, and they were given a routine paste-worming. The paste is squirted into the horses' mouths to destroy any worms in their systems. I was told that all the horses had been done — except Ben.

"Why is that?" I asked.

"He wouldn't let us."

When a horse raises his head and you have your arms extended towards his mouth, you are not far from those front feet, and if you think the hind feet are dangerous, a horse who is good with his front feet is just as dangerous. No one likes to be exposed like that.

Big Ben executes a jump-
off turn.
(Jayne Huddleston)

I was home for a few days between the National Horse Show in New York and the Royal Winter Fair in Toronto. I said, "Is that a fact? Let's worm this horse." I got the job done, with help. Since Ben's tactic was to put his head up as high as he could (and that's very high), we moved him into a section of the barn with a lower ceiling. This very, very strong-willed horse was not trying to hurt us; he simply did not want this worming procedure to happen. Big Ben would perhaps hurt someone if he were surprised or roughly handled, but he is not at all mean by nature. He has never hurt me, but he has hurt others — only because he does not know his own strength.

I remember once coming back from Calgary with a stopover in Winnipeg; the horses had been on the truck for a total of fifty-seven hours. They were all put in their stalls and allowed to settle in for a while. After they were given a bran mash, they had their temperatures taken — rectally, of course. I happened to be walking down the barn aisle and I saw our head girl at that time, Patty Markell, go into Ben's stall to take his temperature. All this registered. It was a picture I saw out of the corner of my eye: Ben eating his bran mash and Patty walking into the stall with the thermometer. It was like one of those puzzles that pose the question, "What's wrong with this picture?" All of a sudden it occurred to me: Big Ben does not want his temperature taken while he is eating his dinner. I immediately turned on my heel and said, "No, Patty." As she turned and stepped back, Big Ben also turned and kicked the wall where Patty had been standing a split second before. If you have never heard the sound of an angry horse kicking a stall wall, imagine a gun going off indoors. He would not have meant to hurt her; it was just his way of saying, "I don't want this done while I'm eating my dinner after fifty-seven hours on a truck."

On another occasion a groom was doing what we call "night check", in which we top up the horses' water, give them some hay, and ensure that all is well. Big Ben was standing with his hind quarters to the stall door, clearly asleep. The groom went to step in with the hay and Big Ben

awoke suddenly and kicked him right out of the stall; the groom ended up sitting out in the aisle with the hay in his lap. I know the horse so well that I could have predicted that response; but I also always sense the mood of any horse before I barge into his stall. That stall is where he lives. A horse is not like a motorcycle that you walk up to and kick-start. The horse's body language says it all. I find it difficult to explain, but just looking at a horse – especially a horse I know – says a lot to me.

When we first got him, Big Ben was not a "people" horse. He tolerated people because they fed him and brought him water, but he did not *like* people at all. During his six years at Millar Brooke Farm, a total of four people have looked after him: Patty Markell, Bobbie Donaher (they have since married), Lori Green, and since 1987, Sandi Patterson. Those four grooms have made him into a people horse by spending countless hours with him, cajoling him. It is their accomplishment, and partly mine. Does he love all people now? No. He is not that type of horse. But, selectively Big Ben really likes certain people, Sandi above all. The horse is very important to her, and no doubt a part of his success belongs to those who care so well for him.

When I acquired him in 1983 I was not concerned with Big Ben's interpersonal skills. I wanted to know what kind of jumper he was going to be. After the Royal Winter Fair in Toronto I started riding and training him, first at home and then in Florida. Originally a kind of training camp for riders and horses, but now quite prestigious, the Florida circuit has expanded to six or seven weeks. That year there were shows in West Palm Beach and Tampa, and I entered him in the preliminary jumper division. I was spending a lot of time on Big Ben, and, of course, many people noticed him. People in the sport tend to talk about horses, what they do well, how they look. Buying a new horse is like buying a new car: you expect questions or compliments. Throughout the Florida circuit, only one person said anything about Big Ben. That was Mark Leone, one of three American brothers who compete in show jumping. All he said was, "He sure is big."

Big Ben is by nature persistent about the things he does not want to do. He has always been a wonderful jumper: the ability, the natural gaits were there. However, because big long strides come easier to him, he much prefers them. Where most horses would cover twelve feet in one canter stride, Big Ben will easily cover fourteen feet. To coax him into the right attitude and the right mood to shorten and compress his stride was step number one. Step number two called for refining and developing the skill to take and hold the short stride. I spent a great deal of time on that.

In the meantime, I was gaining more insight into the horse himself. I soon discovered, for example, what extraordinary eyesight he has. One day I was riding him in a field with trees at one end. He decided he was not going near those trees. I could not for the life of me see what his problem was. I was searching, searching, searching in the trees. Suddenly I spotted a squirrel peeking around the trunk of a tree, looking at us. That tiny creature was the cause of Big Ben's antics. With his acute eyesight he saw everything, and his concentration was easily thrown off. If he saw something he did not like, he would spook. His keen eyes were a gift, but his use of them was sometimes bothersome.

If a large bird was flying a little low, Ben would look up. I have *never* had a horse look up and take exception to a bird. At the horse shows, it was never anything high on the jump that rattled him. Instead, it was a funny-coloured gate, or the rail around the ring, or a sponsor's banner. He was not afraid; he fears very few things. But allowing himself to be rattled by these things was his method of evasion, his way of saying, "I don't want to be trained, I don't want to be controlled." He continued these evasive tactics all the time we were in Florida. He hardly knocked down any jumps. Jumps were never the problem. Convincing this belligerent, willful, and aggressive animal to even consider the possibility that I, his rider, might have a good idea: *that* was the problem.

I look back on the early days with Big Ben and I am grateful that we came together. Others have wondered whether this horse would have enjoyed such success had he landed with someone other than me; but this match made in heaven had a sometimes rocky beginning. Training him was like dealing with a leather-jacketed sixteen-year-old on the edge of becoming a hard case. It could have gone either way.

In training horses, I am always loathe to escalate things. My training method is like water dripping on a stone; I want to avoid at all costs simply reaching for a bigger hammer. I prefer to repeat and repeat and repeat. So, I kept repeating the lesson, and Big Ben kept repeating his evasive tactics. If he spooked or shied at something, I would immediately go to a circle and start working past whatever was bothering him. We would do transitions in and out of the walk, trot, and canter, and just

Big Ben in his paddock at Millar Brooke Farm
(Jayne Huddleston)

through repetition I would make him concentrate on the lesson until he accepted it.

When the Florida circuit ended, we returned home to Perth, and Eve Mainwaring came one day to ride Big Ben. By now we had had him four and half months. I was sitting up in the office, looking through the large window onto the indoor arena, so that I was able to watch Eve on Big Ben. He decided to spook at something, and she gave him a good smart slap with her stick. I thought, "Oh-oh, this is not good." But I was not about to interfere: Eve is a top-of-the-line horsewoman, an outstanding rider, and as my partner in Ben, she had certain rights. I decided I would sit and watch for a while. In a few more minutes he spooked at something else; she gave him another slap. Inside of ten minutes he was all business, going around the arena, not looking at anything. And I thought, "Isn't that interesting? Have I ever learned a lesson today."

When I first began to ride and train Big Ben I had had no doubt that repetition was the correct training technique. But the horse had changed; he had progressed to the point where repetition no longer worked. His belligerence and aggression were sufficiently contained that I could now in fact say to him, "No, you're wrong. You will do it this way now." He was ready to accept this, but I had somehow missed the signal. Eve, the minute she rode him, sensed that he had made this transition and needed a different approach. Two heads are indeed better than one.

9 7

A few weeks later he walked into the ring for a small class at Montreal — new jumps and a new ring, in the past always a big deal for him. He cantered around the ring and over the jumps as though he had been doing it all his life. Every class was like that. A week later we went to Edmonton, and I put him in the preliminary class, with the same success. The next day I moved him up to the intermediate class. Same thing. The next day the open jumper class. Again, the same thing. Finally, on the Sunday, I put him in the grand prix and we came in second. The next week we went to Spruce Meadows in Calgary. I put him in the grand prix there and we won.

That was 1984. He has been a grand prix horse ever since. Only rarely will a horse move up through the ranks that fast. He was like a rocket taking off. What enabled him to do it were his tremendous physical abilities, coupled with the braveness that all great horses possess. Even a horse with such natural ability will lose heart if all of a sudden the jumps get high and wide. The escalation did not bother Big Ben. Since he is such a powerful horse, it was easier for him than for a lot of others.

When I first started riding him faster in jump-offs, I was amazed at his ability to work out of a big pace — to jump from a long, galloping stride and still be accurate and agile and quick. I never imagined that he would be as fast as he is.

Ben showed such promise that we began to consider him for the Los Angeles Olympics in 1984, if Warrior, my leading horse at the time, did not recover from a muscle injury to his hindquarters. In fact, Big Ben came on so strong in the trials for those Games that, despite his relative inexperience, choosing between the two horses was difficult. We ended by taking both and making the decision at the last minute. Big Ben got the nod. He was not in anyone's mind a threat for an individual medal because he lacked sophistication. The hope was that he would be a good team entry. As it turned out in the Nation's Cup competition (the team came in fourth), he was the best Canadian entry of the day.

From that point, we never looked back. The horse has just won and won and won. If anything he gets better, because his mind gets better. He has learned subtleties that many horses would not learn. He learns so quickly that we have had to ensure that he was taught the right thing, because if he ever misunderstood my message, I would be a long time "unteaching" him. On his own, Big Ben arrives at ways to do things more efficiently. I put him in the show ring environment and he learns from that environment. I have never ridden another horse like that.

Such a big horse should actually not be competing in small indoor rings. Big Ben's first indoor circuit exhausted him. Now an indoor circuit is like a walk in the park for him. He is as clever as any horse I have seen

Big Ben jumping at the Los Angeles Olympic Games
(Athlete Information Bureau/ Canadian Olympic Association Photo)

and has by far the best memory. Another thing: he warms up fast. Most riders might jump twenty fences to prepare for the ring. On Big Ben I jump maybe six or eight. There is nothing to it.

He has also learned to behave himself during presentation ceremonies. At first he enjoyed sidling up to other horses just to aim a kick at them. He was more mischief than meanness. The music and spotlights used to drive him wild, and on several occasions he came close to tossing me off. He is calmer now about all of that, and though he will never be like Warrior—who used to *love* a parade—he tolerates the pomp and ceremony.

I see him as a consummate professional who knows his job and does it well. People ask if Big Ben likes me. Yes, I say, and I like him. We are partners and friends and he works for me. But he respects that I am the boss. I do not consider him a pet.

Throughout the years, Big Ben has maintained his ego as well as his playfulness. If I am away, for example, and he has to be ridden to stay in shape, even good riders find him underachieving. The riders, realizing they are on this million-dollar horse, are intimidated, and Big Ben knows it. They think, "This is the mighty Big Ben, and he's behaving badly, but what can I do? I can't hit him." Ben senses this in a heartbeat, and then he is in control. It is amazing to watch, like a mischievous child running amok with his nanny. Mario Deslauriers, a former student of mine and a very competitive rider, is one who *can* ride him. Mario is intimidated by nothing, and Ben knows that. For Mario, he behaves.

Big Ben in the 1986 World Championships in Aachen, West Germany.
(Jayne Huddleston)

Ben can also spot vets and blacksmiths a mile away. Five people identically dressed could visit his stall and Big Ben would let everyone but the real vet or blacksmith among the five lift his foot.

Big Ben loves to compete. Naturally enough, at horse shows he is often the centre of attention. Part of Sandi's job is to protect him from the adoring crowds who seek him out. We were at a show once and so many people had come to see Big Ben that she feared the fuss would affect his performance in the ring. She put up a sign on the stall that read:

> Hi. I'm Big Ben. Glad to have you here. But I'm tired right now. Hope you understand.
>
> — *Big Ben*

At another show, a crowd had gathered around one of Mario's horses, mistaking him for Big Ben. Mario's groom posted a sign on the stall that read, "I'm not Big Ben. He's down the hall."

It is not difficult to understand Big Ben's popularity. His unique size, consistent success, and longevity in the sport have all led to his high profile in Canada, the United States, and Europe. Sandi once put black hoof oil on his shoes, had Big Ben put his foot down on paper, and offered the result as his autograph to satisfy a request. He inspires that kind of affection. Even his old shoes are much sought-after keepsakes.

After the Seoul Olympics in 1988 one long-time correspondent insisted in her letter that sabotage was to blame for our lack of success. Why, she wrote, did I not sleep in the stall with Big Ben? Sometimes people travel a great distance just to see him at the farm. One day an entire busload of his admirers from Kansas turned up.

Young riders from all over the world write eight to ten letters a week to Ben at Millar Brooke, wanting to know his likes and dislikes, his favourite foods, something of his personality. Sandi tells visitors that he is an intelligent, careful horse who doesn't like surprises — green garbage bags blowing in the wind especially irritate him because they can blow

(Above) Paula Heinemann
(in stripes) takes a tour
around the Millar Brooke
Farm barn
(Jayne Huddleston)

(Left) Big Ben, following a
victory at Spruce
Meadows
(Jayne Huddleston)

suddenly in his direction. She will point out that he loves to have a fan directed on him in hot weather, loves children more than adults most of the time, and loves bran muffins any time.

I see him as an extraordinary horse who has the great gift common to all extraordinary horses — generosity. The generous horse tries to win in the ring every bit as much as I do, even though the horse may not understand the concept of winning. He tries his utmost to please me, to cover for my mistakes as much as I cover for his, and he never gives up, despite difficulties. All that is generosity.

On three occasions Big Ben's generosity was severely tested and I came to see how truly great and generous he is: the Pan-American Games in 1987, and the World Cup Finals in 1988 and again in 1989.

CHAPTER 7

Big Ben Tested

On the Pan-American Games medal podium in 1987
(Jayne Huddleston)

Show jumping is one of the few sports in the world that requires the cooperation of two athletes for success, one of them an animal who outweighs his human rider by a thousand pounds or more. Immediately, then, a second set of variables is introduced. The chances of success, especially at the grand prix level, are slim. When horse and rider win at that level, they enjoy a sweet moment when all the variables — footing in the ring, the rider's focus (that word again), the chemistry between horse and rider, luck of the draw (there are advantages to going last), position of the sun (in an outdoor ring), luck itself (and sometimes especially luck) — work in their favour.

If a horse and rider win three grand prix competitions out of twenty over the course of a year, they are doing very well indeed. When I look back on some of Big Ben's more memorable victories, I can still savour those sweet moments. I can call them up, like videos in my head, at will. I can remember each course, every fence, and especially every rail down.

With broadcaster Fred Davis, spokesman for du Maurier, after Big Ben and I won the $250,000 du Maurier International in 1987.
(Andy Rose)

I remember particular events when his brilliance shone — a blistering jump-off one year in a grand prix at Madison Square Garden in New York, when he made an inside cut — a sharp, bravely executed turn — that no other horse had tried to do. Or in 1987, when he won the du Maurier International at Spruce Meadows in Calgary — still the most lucrative show-jumping prize in the world.

I can especially recall when Big Ben won under adverse conditions, for this is the true test of greatness. And when we did not win a medal at the 1988 Olympic Games in Seoul, I can ponder the reasons. But dwell on them? Grow bitter thinking about them? No. There are no sure things in show jumping. There are great expectations, but only so many great rides in the often brief time span that horse and rider are together.

We knew from the outset that Big Ben had the makings of a great horse. But how great? Would his talent and gift for learning be matched by his generosity?

The first test of that spirit of generosity came in the summer of 1987, at the Pan-American Games held in Indianapolis. I remember how incredibly hot it was. Big Ben had been jumping wonderfully. I had ridden him that morning, and he was fine in every respect. Lynn and I watched a few horses compete before us, and then our turn approached. Sandi led Big Ben, and as she turned him around, just the way he turned told me that something was amiss. I did not like one step, the way he moved one leg behind.

"Lynn, did you see that?" I asked.

"I sure did," she agreed.

"Sandi," I said, "Can you walk him forward a little?" She did. He was lame. Fifteen minutes from entering the ring for the first round of the

*Discussing strategy with
Tom Gayford*
(Andy Rose)

Pan-American Games and Big Ben is lame. The stress I felt as the seconds ticked on is impossible to describe.

We called the vet right away. Nothing could be seen on the leg, no swelling, no heat, no cuts. Sandi could recall no incident in the barn. Given that, we had to assume the problem lay in the foot. Straight to the blacksmith we went. At this point we had ten minutes left. The blacksmith pulled off the shoe and, using a hoof tester (a device that applies pressure to the hoof), we attempted to locate a sore area. Sure enough, Big Ben pulled his foot back when one spot was tested. Normally, this would indicate an abscess. If a horse has stepped on a stone (which might have happened weeks before), bruising or perhaps internal bleeding can occur under the sole. Usually the horse's immune system can cope. If not, an infection, or abscess, results. Pus and pressure build up, causing discomfort.

What was to be done? The blacksmith slapped the shoe back on as we stood and watched. Our *chef d'équipe*, Tom Gayford, and I exchanged glances. If Big Ben worked despite the abscess, it would cause him discomfort but not long-term damage. This was not a case of an injury to a ligament or a damaged joint. At worst he might not jump well that day. In our favour was the sandy and soft footing.

I thought to myself, the sport horse in one sense leads a pampered life. We *mow* his paddock for him at home so the grass will be just right. Sandi sleeps outside Big Ben's stall at big events. He travels on airplanes to reduce the time he spends in the trailer. He is well fed and looked after. Nothing is too much for this horse. And for all that, we ask him to work for fifteen minutes when his foot is a little sore. Is that a rationalization? Is it cruel to ask a horse to work under these cir-

Meeting the press as I stepped off Big Ben after winning the individual gold medal at the Pan-American Games.
(Jayne Huddleston)

cumstances when he is not in a position to make the decision for himself? Some might say so.

I do not. Show jumping is a team sport; I have come to believe that a horse *wants* to jump under these circumstances, that a competitive instinct prevails over his sense of discomfort. Had it been an ordinary grand prix event, we would have kept Big Ben in his stall. But we were also sure that without him the Canadian team was out of a medal at these Pan-American Games. In our judgement, he was tough enough and strong enough to jump — and without risking any long-term damage. If I had it to do all over again, I would do the same thing.

I got back on him. He literally warmed to the task at hand, and as his adrenalin started to pump — he is a sensitive, excitable horse, remember — he reacted like an athlete gearing up for battle, and whatever pain he felt bothered him less and less. Instead of planting his foot squarely, he placed his weight more on the toe of that sore foot. In the ring he performed excellently; we placed fifth. He had one unlucky rail, but the time was fast. Given the circumstances, the performance was very good.

That night I borrowed a horse from the mounted police unit for the presentation ceremony, because, after the day's round, and after standing on the foot, Big Ben was now quite uncomfortable. He stayed right up on his toe, not wanting to put his weight down on the heel.

Back in the barn, we took off his shoe and had him stand in a tub of water and Epsom salts — as hot as he could bear. Uncooperative about this, of course, he would keep his foot in the water for thirty or forty seconds and then get bored and take it out. This continued from 5:30 to about 10:30. I spent a great deal of time putting his foot back in the water, because he knows me and lets me do with him certain things he will not let others do.

Every half hour, between soakings, we put on his foot something called an Easy Boot, a plastic overshoe that covers the whole foot. We walked him on the asphalt, which produces a percussive effect that stimulates the abscess. About 10:30 that night we used a bran poultice in an attempt to draw the abscess.

Meanwhile a subplot to the story began to unfold, and it upset me greatly. At the Games was an American vet named Danny Marks, one of the top sport-horse veterinarians in the world and a specialist in sports injury. Often at international competitions the Canadians share the costs of a vet with the Americans. (The Canadian team always seems to be short of money for these things.) But in this case, we had thought, "We're just going down to Indianapolis; what can go wrong?" Lacking the necessary funds, we had not made a deal with Danny Marks.

Dr. Marks, needless to say, was involved in the treatment of Big Ben. We met the next morning, and he had some bad news.

The team that won the gold medal at the 1987 Pan-American Games. (From right) Hugh Graham, Lisa Carlsen, and Laura Balisky next to me. (Jayne Huddleston)

"Ian," he said, "I don't know how to tell you this, but I can't work on this horse. I have orders from Frank Chapot [the *chef d'équipe* of the American team] not to work on this horse any more." We were outraged, absolutely outraged. Frank Chapot was arguing, I suppose, that because we had no contractual arrangement, Dr. Marks was not obligated to work on Big Ben. He knew that Big Ben ranked as a real threat for a medal. The Americans had come to the Games believing they would win the whole thing handily, but they had appeared a little shaky the first day.

I argued my case as best I could.

"But Danny, you've flown up to Millar Brooke Farm on several occasions. You've worked for us in Florida, in New York, in Europe — on a one-to-one basis. I'm a client of the Delaware Equine Clinic, where you practise." And certainly payment for his services was not the issue.

"I know all that," he said. "But I can't work on your horse any more at these Pan-American Games. I'm sorry."

During the course of the day, three of the four riders on the American show-jumping team came to me and said, "We want you to know we had nothing to do with this decision."

All this was troubling, and not at all typical of the sport. The vast majority of international riders want to beat each other in the ring, and only in the ring. They don't cling to technicalities if another competitor is having difficulties. I remember one year at the Royal Winter Fair in Toronto, a Canadian rider had a fall in the first class and retired from the competition with a shoulder injury. Facing disaster because the Nations' Cup loomed the next day, our *chef d'équipe* made the rounds of the other teams and asked if they would permit a substitute. The rules normally forbid substitution to avoid the following scenario: a horse has an off day, his rider feigns injury, and the *chef d'équipe* brings in a substitute horse-and-rider combination. However, a jury and an organizing committee may permit substitution if the other *chefs d'équipe* do not object; of course, they did not object on this occasion.

No vet, then, for Big Ben. On the other hand, Dr. Marks had already done as much as he could have done. Now we were on our own. We took Big Ben to the blacksmith shop. The building had a cement floor with a rubber mat in the middle where the horses could stand. Ben, by now at the end of his patience, would let neither the blacksmith nor any of his co-workers pick up his foot to put on a new shoe. In ten minutes, I could see, it would turn into a brawl. Big Ben would not be intimidated by these big, strong blacksmiths.

Time marched on and the Nations' Cup event edged closer. I told the blacksmiths that sometimes with this horse the stall is the best place to accomplish a task. Maybe in the stall Ben would let Sandi lift the foot. They were willing to try anything. Back to the stall. Because the weather was so hot, and because Big Ben likes fans on him, we had one in the corner. Amy, then ten, was holding his head close to the fan and feeding him carrots.

Sandi walked into the stall, ran her hand down the horse's right hind leg, and said simply, "Lift your foot, Bennie." Which he did, as naturally as can be. The blacksmith, an excellent blacksmith named H. R. Kaplan, seized the moment. Normally a blacksmith working on that leg would position himself alongside the horse, with his back to the horse's head. But in this case Sandi occupied that position while holding Big Ben's foot. H. R. Kaplan stood behind the horse, facing the back of the horse. I never saw anything like it. And he popped the shoe on *so* fast. Most blacksmiths take a long time to get a shoe on; he had that shoe on in less than a minute — a remarkable piece of work.

Still the horse was not comfortable. I mounted him and he seemed better than the previous day, but not completely correct. Nevertheless, he went in the ring and jumped a clean round in the Nations' Cup.

As we were walking out of the ring, Lynn said, "Look!"

On the coronet band, which is where the hoof meets the hair of the leg, I could see a little rupture the size of a nickel in the skin, emanating pus. The abscess had come out the *top* of the foot, which is unusual. At some point during the round, the abscess had popped, releasing the pressure, and the horse was perfectly sound. Later Big Ben jumped another clean round, contributing to the team gold for Canada. On the last day he won the whole thing — individual gold — and competed in the next tournament.

Big Ben and I left the Pan-American Games with two gold medals. That was special: to win under circumstances that would have stopped most horses.

His spirit was illustrated once more at the 1988 World Cup Final held in Göteborg, Sweden. There was a virus going around that year knocking horses out of commission. Some horses did not truly recover for six months; others got over it in two or three weeks. Big Ben had been exposed to the virus during the winter circuit in Florida before going to Sweden. We arrived in Sweden, and he seemed fine. He won the first leg of the finals, and did fairly well the next day. But following the second leg of the competition, he began to show signs of colic, a potentially dangerous internal problem, which is extremely rare for him. His temperature also ran high. Strict rules would not allow medication.

On Big Ben, winning our first World Cup in 1988 in Göteborg, Sweden.
(Maarten Jurgens)

Sandi Patterson escorts Big Ben to the presentation ceremony at the 1988 World Cup Final.
(Maarten Jurgens)

Fortunately, we got a rest day, Saturday, before the final leg of the event, which featured two rough grand prix tests over huge jumps. On the rest day I merely walked him. I knew, Lynn knew, the vet knew he was in trouble – not dying of this virus, but not feeling well either.

Sunday came. At this point I led in the standings. Talk about having one foot on a banana peel. Though not right, Big Ben somehow jumped a four-fault first round, and we still held the lead going into the last round. This was the toughest one, because now Big Ben was really tired. It took every bit of juice he had to do the job. Not his light, scopey (powerful) self, he nevertheless jumped a clean round – good enough to win the World Cup Final of 1988. Within three weeks, Big Ben felt well again. The virus, it seemed, had been defeated.

After the disappointment of the 1988 Olympics in Seoul, Korea, the 1989 World Cup event held in Tampa, Florida, provoked a fresh round of anticipation. For many people the big question was, "Will Big Ben and

The victory gallop after our World Cup win in Göteborg.
(Jayne Huddleston)

Ian repeat as champions?'' John Quirk, the knowledgeable editor of *Horses*, an American magazine, asked me, "Is Big Ben really back?" I told him that Big Ben was not coming back, because he had never left. A combination of circumstances had thrown him off form for a week in his life at the time of the Olympics. One of the frustrating things about our sport, I remind myself, is that it is completely unpredictable. Peaking horses is an inexact science.

But in Tampa we got it right, and Ben showed what he could do when all the variables mesh. Held annually, the World Cup Final gathers the top horse-and-rider combinations, which then jump three times against each other. Riders rarely win more than one class; the quality is too high. But we did win, and in unprecedented fashion, establishing a number of firsts: Big Ben was the first horse – and we were the first horse-and-rider combination – to win back-to-back World Cup Finals, and Big Ben was the first horse ever to win two consecutive World Cup Finals. We were also the first horse-and-rider combination to win all three phases of the World Cup. These are things that may never happen again in World Cup competition.

Everything came up roses. If we hit a rail, it bounced and went back in the cups. I felt like a proud parent. Rarely have I ridden a horse that I thought was a better horse than I am a rider. But that week at Tampa in 1989 Big Ben showed himself the exception to the rule. The courses presented major difficulties; Bert de Nemethy is one of the best course designers in the world, and he tested and investigated every horse's and every rider's strengths and weaknesses. No horse ever backs into a World Cup victory.

At the press conference following the 1989 World Cup in Tampa
(Tish Quirk)

Imagine a horse race. Big Ben crosses the wire, and the rest are back five lengths trying to decide who is second. That week he stood in a class by himself. When the competition ended, he was given a standing ovation. And the people cheered for him, not me. At the press conference afterwards I said, "Look, you've got to understand that all I did was escort this horse around the courses. The hero here is Big Ben." I am normally loathe to create any impression that in show jumping the rider is a mere passenger, less than an elite athlete, that it is all the horse's doing; but on this day I did indeed feel like a passenger, and a privileged one.

Big Ben is owned by some twenty-five different people and groups, and many of them were in Tampa for the competition. They went wild. Standing around in a group back in the barn, some of us in tears, we all told each other what we felt at that moment. This very moving exchange was recorded on film by Vid Laurusaitis. Well known in show-jumping circles for his video business, Vid normally records riders in competition who may want to learn by watching their mistakes, or perhaps they want to bask in a moment of glory. That day in Tampa he recorded pure joy.

The next morning we headed back to Canada. Lynn and I took the truck, with the camper trailing behind. Someone else drove the horse van, with Sandi and Big Ben inside. Lynn flipped through newspapers with coverage of the World Cup, intending to read them aloud; but she dissolved into tears, unable to continue reading. Extraordinary things were written about Big Ben. Journalists called Big Ben "perfection in motion". John Quirk, the same writer who had wondered if Big Ben was back, called the win "an accomplishment for the ages". I thought, "Maybe I should retire now?" The victory hardly seemed real. And how would it ever be topped?

In all my competitive life, I had never tasted victory so sweet. I may never see the like of it again.

But that moment of triumph did not compensate for, or erase the disappointment of not winning in September at the 1988 Seoul Olympics. Before every competition, but especially the big ones, I have the team – vet, blacksmith, groom, trainer – prepare the horses as best they can. But there is no predicting when all of that preparation will come together. All my expertise as a rider and trainer can only limit the downside: some days we are destined to win, others not.

I knew very early on during the Olympics that victory was not in the cards. The individual competition featured a five-round formula, and I knew on day one how the rest would unfold. There were not going to be any miracles for me in that elegant setting created by Olaf Peterson. The course designer had taken dragons and gardens, themes from Korean

culture, to design a course of jumps whose like I had never seen before. Only in retrospect would I appreciate the course's esthetic appeal.

I had a feeling long before going to Korea. At Millar Brooke, after I had schooled Big Ben several times, Lynn and I began to have concerns. We reviewed those concerns with Dr. Atack, Ben's vet, Lewis Forest, his blacksmith, and Tom Gayford. We repeatedly screened videos from his last few competitions, until we began to wonder if we were imagining things. Were we looking for problems where problems did not exist? Instinct more than anything told me that something felt wrong: Big Ben was not reacting to training as he should have. I caught a little hint in his attitude, yet there was nothing we could really pinpoint.

On Big Ben in Seoul. Course designer Olaf Peterson created magnificent obstacles based on themes from Korean culture and mythology. Big Ben is leaping an ornate triple bar.
(Tish Quirk)

113

Canada's show-jumping team at the Seoul Olympics, 1988. Mario Deslauriers and John Anderson are on my left. Seated are Lisa Carlsen (left) and Laura Balisky.
(Jayne Huddleston)

In Korea the footing in the ring did not suit him. Nothing came easily. I was forced to ride Big Ben differently: my preferred style is subtly to orchestrate the horse's performance in the ring. If I appear to be doing little, that is by design. The greatest compliment anyone could pay me would be to call me an efficient rider. I try to help the horse maximize his ability, keeping everything as simple as possible. If I am other than a quiet rider in the ring – if I ride the way I did at the '88 Olympics – then something is not right with the horse.

Horse people understand that it was not our week in Seoul. They would not have been surprised had we gone home and won the next five grand prix in a row. People outside the horse world do not see it that way. They see Ian Millar and Big Ben among the favourites for a medal. But even a favourite horse-and-rider combination has odds of winning of perhaps ten to one. In our sport, victory is never certain. There is an X factor, an element of mystery or magic that stems from the need to peak two world-class athletes – the horse and the rider – at precisely the same moment.

I knew all that. Nonetheless, I was profoundly disappointed, especially in the twenty-four hours following the loss. Disappointed for Lynn and for myself, but more for our shareholders and all the people in

Watching the entry ahead of me and waiting my turn in Seoul.
(Athlete Information Bureau/ Canadian Olympic Association Photo)

Canada who had such high hopes for us. I knew I had not let anybody down; the horse had not let anybody down. It simply was not meant to be. What keeps me sane in my sport is a philosophical attitude. When a competition does not go right, I analyse it to death, and learn from it, but then I put it away before moving on to the next competition, because if I allow disappointment to carry forward, that emotion is going to get in my way.

There remains, however, one possible explanation for Big Ben's performance at Seoul: the virus that afflicted some horses at the Tampa showgrounds prior to the 1988 World Cup in Sweden. Many horses succumbed. Symptoms included high temperature, loss of energy, some swelling in the legs. After treatment using broad-spectrum antibiotics, the virus would appear to go away. Equine viral anemia (E.V.A.). was suspected. Of our two horses at the World Cup, the mare Future Shock became ill immediately and recovered just as quickly; Big Ben developed

At the Seoul Olympics
(Tish Quirk)

symptoms of colic. He had a temperature, a little swelling in his legs, and he was not himself. He was, however, able to finish (and win) the competition.

On the Monday following the World Cup victory, the vets had even had some concerns about putting Big Ben on a plane. We had finally brought him home, apparently recovered, but only after quarantine and an additional two weeks' rest in New York. Throughout that summer he had competed, but not rigorously, with a good break before Korea. If I suspect anything about his poor Olympic performance, I would say that Big Ben had not completely shaken off that viral infection. Perhaps the stress of the trip was to blame. Known to lose 150 pounds from shipping and to take three weeks to recover the lost weight, Big Ben is only an adequate traveller. Was the heat of a long summer to blame?

Big Ben, if he could talk, would tell us and explain the mystery. But as smart as he is and as great as he is, talking is one thing Big Ben cannot do.

I often think of what the man in that arena in Belgium said about Big Ben. "Too big, too ugly." Ugly is perhaps extreme. Very skinny then, he did have trouble keeping weight on, but even fleshed out, he does not possess classic beauty: his body angles are severe. When I think of a beautiful horse I think of all the curves and angles flowing together the way they do in a handsome human figure. When Big Ben enters the show ring he does not impress with his beauty. His winning record, not his good looks, assures his celebrity status on both sides of the Atlantic.

In December of 1989, I competed with Big Ben in Brussels. We had just come from Bordeaux, France, where he had jumped exceedingly well to win that grand prix, after claiming the one in Stuttgart, West Germany, a few weeks beforehand. Coming to Belgium, his birthplace, and right after such great victories and an even greater year, was very much a case of the native son returning home to a tumultuous welcome. His World Cup victories, along with all his other great wins, have made this Belgian-bred horse very special in Belgium.

During the competition, I learned that a nationally televised presentation for Big Ben was to take place on one of the evenings. The ceremony began with me riding around the ring on Big Ben, expecting something, but not quite sure what. While the announcer talked in Flemish and French, the spotlight suddenly turned to the in-gate, where a small chestnut mare was being led into the ring. The mare struck me as very correct in her build and conformation, though certainly not pretty. I realized immediately that this was Oekie, Big Ben's mother. In the background I could see another horse coming — a big, strong-looking stallion. I recognized his look. This was Etretat, Ben's father. Ben looked

Giving Big Ben my special congratulatory pat just moments after he jumped his gold-medal-winning performance at the Pan-American Games of 1987.
(Jayne Huddleston)

at them and nickered, his head raised up, his ears pricked forward. All the while he looked straight at the mare. Had he recognized his mother? It is highly unusual for Ben to look at another horse and nicker like that.

With Big Ben flanked by his mother and father, I was formally presented with an oil painting of Etretat. The subject of the painting, meanwhile, took a look at his offspring and tried to kick him. The crowd responded first with laughter, then with tears. By the time the announcers finished speaking, everyone in the arena had been touched in some way. It was an unforgettable moment for me and for the Belgian people, who are avid followers of the sport and for whom Big Ben has heroic stature.

I have had seventeen or eighteen grand prix horses in my career, but Big Ben may be that one-in-a-lifetime horse. My habit after riding with Big Ben in competition is to reach over with my right hand and pat the left side of his neck. It's not something I do consciously, yet I seem to do it only with very special horses. I imagine I will be doing that with Big Ben for a few years to come.

When he finally retires and is put out to pasture at Millar Brooke Farm, he will have earned his leisure many times over.

CHAPTER 8

On the Road to Spruce Meadows

*S*eptember 9, 1989. Saturday, day four of the Spruce Meadows Masters show-jumping tournament in the foothills just south of Calgary, Alberta. For the size of its purses (in 1989 worth more than $1 million) and for the Olympic-class competition that such prize money draws, Spruce Meadows is world-famous. But among riders and veteran spectators, the event's weather has become a long-standing joke.

When riders compete elsewhere and the weather turns sour, they may laugh and claim to be practising for Spruce Meadows.

With Tom Gayford and his daughter Margie, who is dressed for the unseasonably cold Spruce Meadows weather on an early September day.
(Andy Rose)

Marg Southern, who co-chairs Spruce Meadows
(Andy Rose)

The "whipper-in" operating the in-gate at the All-Canada, or national, ring (he is like an usher with a microphone, ensuring that horse-and-rider combinations are ready to enter the ring according to "the order of go") has taken to wearing a toque over his headphones. Children among the spectators some days wrap themselves in blankets, and at the Equi-Fair—a huge tent with a convention-like feel, where horse-related and other products are sold—there is a brisk trade in ski jackets.

"Don't like our weather?" I heard Marg Southern, who co-chairs the competition, say one day. "Wait five minutes." The first day the sun was strong enough to inflict sunburn; now there is talk of snow. When a young marching band, including girls with bare legs, made its first of many entries into the international show ring, some wit remarked that their white safari hats were at least useful in keeping off the hail. Yes, the hail has been and gone.

But the weather is no deterrent. Twelve nations are represented, with 144 riders and 278 horses. There are Olympic gold medalists, World Cup champions, European champions, some of the great riders and mounts in the equestrian world. International flags and huge sponsor billboards give a European feel to the classy Spruce Meadows facility. In the seventies, Spruce Meadows co-chairman Ron Southern went to Europe gathering ideas for its design: the clock tower at the in-gate to the international ring is modelled on one in Dublin; the enclosed section on the west side borrowed design elements from Hickstead, a prominent show-jumping venue in England. Adding to the international flavour on the grounds behind the stadium are tents and mini-pavilions where the foods of various nations are sold: Bavarian sausage, Dutch cheese, Australian mineral water.

Out on the international hitching (or warm-up) ring this windswept day I am warming up Big Ben and trying to stay warm myself. To me, show jumping is an outdoor sport, and I prefer the outdoors anyway. Most of the time.

Among grooms and "ground men" (a term for people who, among their many other duties, act as the rider's eyes on the ground) there is the usual jockeying for available practice jumps. Sandi Patterson is adjusting the vertical according to my instructions. Horse traffic is fairly light out here: Jos Lansik of The Netherlands on Felix, Joe Fargis of the United States on Mill Pearl, Thomas Fuchs of Switzerland on Dollar Girl. The wind, the same wind loudly snapping flags on Spruce Meadows flag poles, must come from some peak in the Rockies, and it finds a home in my bones. Sandi is stiff with cold, her arms at her sides.

In a matter of minutes I will take off my red oilskin coat; underneath I wear the red coat worn by members of Canada's show-jumping team. Our focus, mine and Big Ben's, is building, as it must, to those eighty-five seconds in the ring. The foul weather is one Spruce Meadows tradition beyond my control; the other tradition — of the Canadian team never having won the Nations' Cup here — is one I would dearly love to eradicate. In the twelve years the team competition has been held, the British have won it five times and the Americans four times. In its best showings, Canada came second in 1978 and again in 1988. Close, but not good enough.

Joe Fargis, veteran American grand prix rider and winner of both team gold and individual gold medals at the 1984 Los Angeles Olympics

A great rider is one who can do everything that involves horses: break and train them, understand their mentalities and problems, know how fast or how slow to go, and teach them. The job doesn't end with riding. Horseman is an all-encompassing term, and a good rider is a good horseman. A lot of people today are learning to ride. Period. It stops with the riding.

Ian's riding style is classical. There's not a thing unusual about it. That's what makes it so good. It's textbook. Being tall doesn't put him at a disadvantage. I'm tall too. Being tall and having a classical style makes him a more efficient rider. There's more leverage in his body.

We both started riding at the grand prix level at the same time: the fall circuit of 1971. Ian had two at best mediocre horses, and he sure didn't do very well. I saw him a few years later, and I remember thinking to myself how resilient he was. This time he had the horsepower. There's something to resilience.

Big Ben is a very good horse being ridden by a very good rider. The combination makes it way above average. One without the other wouldn't be quite as good.

Ian employs a system. There's nothing exotic or mystical about it. You walk before you run, and if the horse is tired, you don't jump him. For twenty years, nothing has changed in that system. He just keeps on winning.

Big Ben had yesterday off, and he is fresh now. Too fresh, I fear. But I am stopped in this train of thought. A woman with a camera has climbed the white fence meant to separate horses and riders from spectators, and walked out here. Would I, she asks, halt Big Ben and pose for a shot? I oblige. Later, I think how little most North Americans understand about our sport. In Europe, where show jumping is more established, this likely would not have happened. Spectators here are denied access to hockey players about to step on the ice for a game, or baseball players waiting in the on-deck circle; riders about to compete need the same breathing room. As much as I like to see and meet people, fans in the warm-up area are at best a distraction, at worst unsafe.

The Nations' Cup competition works like this: after drawing to determine sequence, each of the seven teams here (Britain, the United States, The Netherlands, Switzerland, West Germany, Mexico, and Canada) sends out its first horse-and-rider combination. Each nation follows along until four combinations from each country have gone. After two rounds, the winning nation is the one with the lowest number of faults among its three best horse-and-rider combinations. In the event of a tie, a jump-off determines the winner.

Tom Gayford, the laid-back *chef d'équipe* of the Canadian team, and a respected but nevertheless under-rated horseman in this country, ranks among the wisest men I know. He is guarded, and it takes time to get to know him. But in difficult judgement calls about horses and riders, or indeed about life in general, he is almost always right. Tom comes from a different era, yet he remains a flexible student of the sport who has made the transition to modern-day show jumping. But you must listen carefully to this very subtle man when he says something. He is not going to spell it out for you. I, on the other hand, will underline it, say it five times, and then ask the person to repeat it back to me to ensure they have understood.

Tom Gayford, team gold medallist in show jumping at the 1968 Olympics and *chef d'équipe* of the Canadian equestrian team

Ian has a farm system of horses, and through his sponsors, they buy young horses, then feed them in, and if they're not good enough, he and his sponsors sell them — they're good for other people. This is why Ian will stay at the top: he's one of the few riders with a farm system. The other riders are trying to buy *horses; Ian is* making *them.*

Ian is very serious and dedicated when the chips are down and the Canadian equestrian team is in the thick of the competition. I can tell how tense he is by how hard he rags on me. Ian has a good sense of humour. One time at a very formal banquet he walked by me and pulled my hair. Only one person would do that; I know who it is. Ian's also a prankster. Riders are given a certain number of free passes to competitions; he'll deny getting his passes, deny I've done this or that when I know exactly what I've done. He'll tell me I put the wrong horse in the class, and insist he had told me something else. He's very light-hearted that way.

Our team success is due to our team spirit, and Ian has a mountain of team spirit. There's nothing reasonable he won't do for the team. He's very good at sharing his knowledge before the team rides in a Nations' Cup. On the other hand, he would never impose himself on another rider.

It's almost unfair the pressure that's on Ian. The kids wanting to see Ben, autograph-hunters, the media. A top athlete has to put up with this. But there are times when we have to run a lot of interference for him, times when he's pushed too far. Ian handles the pressure well. He deals well with his owners. Owners can be tough to talk to when you're tense; he's a smart man and a smart businessman who knows how to talk to his owners.

Once in a while Ian and I will go out for dinner. Just the two of us. We'll walk away from it all. Have a beer and unwind.

A number of things contribute to his success: one is that all this tension building and building inside him is not *conveyed to the horse.*

You can compare Ian to Wayne Gretzky in hockey or back a little bit to Teeder Kennedy and Syl Apps, Jean Beliveau, all the great athletes. Besides natural talent they have the will to win, to stay in condition and perform. Ian even stopped his cigars because he understands this. He understands that at his age he has to spend a little more time staying fit; he exercises his back to protect that weakness he has. After a class — it doesn't matter if it's a green jumper or a grand prix — he analyses and wants to know. *We'll argue over what happened and why. He's ever the student, always looking to improve.*

But he would be nowhere near where he is without Lynn. Lynn is very good in barn management; she keeps the place running. She can handle people and sponsors and take the pressure off, and yet create a home life. She travels with Ian, and she's a very calming influence. Yet she's lots of fun to be with.

Tom Gayford
(Jayne Huddleston)

Ian's a super sportsman and a super guy, and I admire the fact that he's sensitive to other people's feelings. I send my daughters to him for training when I can't be there. There's nobody better in the world.

Watch him ride. There's great enjoyment to be had in watching Ian Millar lay down a perfect trip around the ring.

With Mario Deslauriers
(Mary Jo Ormesher)

Strategy in these Nations' Cups is important. Tom has opted to let Mario Deslauriers, the fine young Québécois rider, go first on Revlon Rascal. Mario was only nineteen when he won the World Cup in 1984, the youngest rider ever to win it. One of his great strengths is his outstanding ability to solve problems in the ring. It is relatively easy to ride around a course when nothing goes wrong; Mario can solve a long list of problems on course and keep a competitive round going at the same time.

By letting Mario go first, Tom takes some of the pressure off less experienced riders Jay Hayes and Harold Chopping, who will go second and third respectively. Watching Mario ride and hearing his comments afterwards will offer some advantage to team riders not accustomed to such intense pressure. I will ride fourth, with luck an ace in the deck and one we may not even have to rely on if the others go well.

The footing this day — and all week — has been difficult. It has rained every night, and most horses do not like the sloppy turf. Mario goes first, and it goes badly. Two rails down: eight faults. Harold fares no better on Aerobic, Jay even worse on Zucarlos. Our turn now. I am wishing that

Mario Deslauriers, Canadian grand prix rider, and the youngest rider ever to win the World Cup

Ian and I have a special relationship. My father taught me a lot about riding, but Ian finished the job. I rode with him for a year and a half; he put polish on my ride. As a teacher, he explains well, and a student can learn a lot just by watching him. When I trained with him, he didn't necessarily want to change my style; he just wanted me to relate to the horse.

He's always looking for something better to teach the horse. He has a wonderful way with them, and he's always asking himself, "How can I make the horse better? How can I be better?"

Ian is very very cool in the ring. That gives him a big edge, the fact that he can control the pressure.

I think Big Ben is good for several more years, but I see Future Vision as the next Big Ben.

The Canadian team at the 1989 Spruce Meadows Masters: (left to right) Jay Hayes, Harold Chopping, Mario Deslauriers, and me, with Tom Gayford in front.
(Jayne Huddleston)

Big Ben were not so fresh. The slippery footing rattles him, but he seems eager nevertheless. Approaching a triple bar on the course – which is tough, a real test – I try to check Big Ben's speed. He replies, in effect, "No, I'm just fine. Let's go." The result is one rail down and four faults. The Canadian team after round one is deep in a hole of its own creation.

Round two starts more promisingly. Mario has four faults, Jay twelve, and Harold holds at eight. Big Ben, now with a little of that freshness taken out of him, calmly jumps a clean round. But it is all too little and much too late. Of the seven teams, Canada comes in dead last.

The British, true to form, are unbeatable. Nick Skelton on Grand Slam has been winning all week in the international ring. He is a shrewd rider and as good a competitor as I have ever seen. Today he has an off day and rings up twelve and eight faults respectively over his two rounds. But the team had no need of him anyway. John Whitaker and his magnificent grey, Milton, jump clear on both rounds, the only ones to do so. The British national anthem is played one more time, then "Radetzky's March" by Johann Strauss Sr. – the signature music of Spruce Meadows – as the British team rides triumphantly around the ring.

For us it is a dismal showing. But win or lose, journalists, including a number from Europe, have questions. The Canadian team is called to a press conference to explain its poor performance. Tom Gayford is disappointed, but refrains from saying so. He mentions the difficulties facing young team riders, young horses. A reporter from the *Calgary Herald* presses him, wondering why certain western riders were left off the team. Tom grows testy at any suggestion that western equestrians have been overlooked in favour of eastern ones. This is an old and long-dead issue, he says, to which I might add, Amen. When the team leaves the press conference, Tom and the reporter are still locked in private combat.

John Whitaker, British grand prix rider and 1989 European Champion

What makes a good rider? First of all, the will to win. Secondly, the best riders know their own and their horse's capabilities and keep within them. Ian has all that. He's a very good judge of a course. When he walks a course he knows it inside out, every possibility, where to take a stride out to save time, what fences he could take risks at. He has a very professional approach. Nothing is left to chance with Ian.

At our level of competition, it's 80 per cent horse, and 20 per cent rider (although many would disagree and argue that it's fifty-fifty). So the ability to choose and train horses is critical. A lot of people who know what they're doing are looking for those great horses. Horses like Big Ben or Milton, these are exceptional horses. Almost freaks. They're superstars, and you need luck to find them. Ian is lucky, but you make your own luck.

I've never seen Ian get rough with a horse or ever show that he's upset. Everybody has a bad round; some people tend to take it out on their horses. It looks bad. You never see Ian blame his horse. A very cool professional, he doesn't fall apart when things go wrong. Horses can have their off days. You see some riders after bad rounds changing bits, changing everything. The Olympic Games in Seoul were probably disappointing for him (they were for me too). His horse was just going through a bad patch, health-wise or whatever. But right after that, Ian won the World Cup. The strong riders, like Ian, put their finger on what went wrong, and the next week they're back there winning.

Ian won all three legs of the World Cup in 1989. I had never seen anyone so determined, and yet so cool. Sometimes determination can take over. You can get too keyed. I'll never forget: he was just about to go in the ring for the last leg, and he asked the coach, Tom Gayford, "What's my slack?" It was a phrase I had never heard before and it made me laugh. I'm sure it meant, "How many fences can I afford to take down?" [His "slack" was two fences.]

What makes Big Ben great is his temperament and his ability. I know of no other horse with as much ability, and for such a big horse, he's so agile. He's fantastic. He just knows a big occasion and he rises to it. That goes with all the top horses. A normal horse will fall apart at the big event; the good horse comes through and gets better.

And with luck, the horse suits the rider. Ian looks like he was born on Big Ben's back. It's a perfect partnership. If somebody else had bought the horse, you might never have heard of him. It's not taking anything away from Big Ben; it's just that the combination is so perfect.

John Whitaker
(Andy Rose)

British chef d'équipe,
Ronnie Massarella
(Jayne Huddleston)

Tomorrow is Sunday, September 10, the day of the du Maurier International, the one class that occupies the thoughts of every eligible rider here.

The prize money for first place in the du Maurier International — $165,000 — makes it the richest grand prix event in the world. But the rules at Spruce Meadows differ from international rules at most other competitions. This year a requirement that both horse *and* rider qualify to compete in the du Maurier International has the British grumbling. At many European shows, only the rider need qualify for the big event by doing well in events leading up to the grand prix — and on his second horses if the rider chooses. There has been a blunder in communications, so that the British arrive thinking one thing, only to learn another.

The British *chef d'équipe*, Ronnie Massarella, raises the matter at a press conference early in the week, and threatens as a protest to sit out some of his top horses from the Nations' Cup. He argues that it asks too much of top horses to make them qualify during the week as well as compete in the team and grand prix events. "We're only thinking of the horses," say the British riders. A tempest is brewing in the Spruce Meadows teapot. Eventually, the British relented and never did carry out their threat.

I had to agree with the British. It struck me that too many riders had been invited to the competition, thus necessitating the qualifying rule. The man behind this mad stampede to compete at Spruce Meadows is Ron Southern. In the world of show jumping, there is no one like him.

An extremely successful businessman, Ron and his wife, Marg, have built Spruce Meadows up from nothing. They began in 1976, a year when no international riders bothered to attend and the prize money totalled a mere $76,000. The Spruce Meadows Masters is now one of the most prestigious competitions in the world. The Southerns have been dynamic contributors to the sport. Their example of running a competition, and of serving corporate sponsors, is without compare. They have also done a tremendous amount to commercialize the sport in Canada — which has to happen if we are to compete consistently with the world's best. Each year, three major show-jumping events, including the Masters in September, take place at Spruce Meadows, whose appeal is undeniable.

Four times during the Masters tournament all international team riders don their red or blue coats — Gerry Mullins, representing Ireland, is conspicuous by his green military uniform — and participate in the "Parade of Nations", which includes a marching band, the King's Troop Royal Horse Artillery, and a small international flotilla. Parachutists drop from the sky, dogs compete in a canine version of show jumping, western

Trying to toss a ball through a hoop in the Spruce Meadows "Mini-Olympics". Gail Greenough (right) is looking on.
(Jayne Huddleston)

riders put on displays of horsemanship: all designed to please the crowd. Lost in this circus atmosphere, say Ron Southern's critics, is show jumping, but by Sunday, grand prix day, the crowds swell to forty thousand or more — a full house. Critics find it hard to argue with that kind of success.

Spruce Meadows is young, but already traditions abound. Last Wednesday night, for example, the riders engaged in amusing, off-horse games. This year it was volleyball between national team members, and Canada won. Other years, three-legged races, baseball, and relay races were on the agenda, all followed by a party and more silliness. Later, under a big-top-tent-become-a-restaurant, each team came to the microphone and, aided by a live band, sang for the entertainment of the several hundred gathered there. The home-made lyrics were satirical or funny; where language or creativity failed them, teams turned to the pop charts. This year the Mexican riders stole the show with their version of "La Bamba"; the Americans ranked as the worst and loudest contraltos. A Dutch rider snatched my Snowy River hat (the same one I would later give away to John Whitaker in Stuttgart) as a prop for his team's musical contribution. Soon enough the tent had the feel of a beer hall. German and Austrian riders with their hands and arms locked swayed to the music. The week of the 1989 Masters was young and full of possibilities.

All this is the Southerns' doing. I sometimes wonder whether I would have the Bank of Montreal as a corporate sponsor without the Southerns' involvement in the sport. The bank became involved with Spruce Meadows first, and then with other shows, before connecting with me through my capable agent, Elliott Kerr. Show jumping in Canada owes a lot to Marg and Ron Southern.

Ron Southern
(Andy Rose)

Ron Southern, co-chairman, Spruce Meadows Show-Jumping Tournaments, Calgary, Alberta

In building Spruce Meadows fourteen years ago, we wanted to create a genuine sport and remove it from the social pages. The happy circumstance was that about that time Ian decided he was going to make a career out of the sport. We created a unique facility for the sport in North America. But it all would have been for nothing had there not been an athlete with the tremendous depth of skills, determination, and expertise that Ian displayed: he became the first hero of show jumping in Canada. He is to our sport in Canada what Jackie Robinson was to baseball in the United States. Without Ian, the sport in Canada would never have gained the credibility that it has today. If the sport is to be successful, it has to be appreciated by people from every walk of life, and part of Ian's great appeal is that he is appreciated and admired by all who make up our broad base of fan support.

This is a tough sport. You have to be superbly conditioned, you need tremendous reflexes, you have to be disciplined, focused, and you have to have an overpowering instinct to win. Ian has all that. And he has super nerves for the sport; that's one of his great attributes. He's able to come through in the crunch. The added bonus with Ian is that he has a wonderful family, and he will become, if he isn't now, the first North American to become a millionaire out of show jumping. He deserves every penny of it. For he has hacked a career out of the sport, committing his total energy to show jumping before it became lucrative.

Ian can see himself as part of a bigger picture. He's perceptive, incisive, statesmanlike in his comments about fans, other athletes, organizers, sponsors, as well as what the sport should be in the future. Most people can't do that. Wayne Gretzky and a very few other athletes can do it. That's what makes these people remarkable.

Ian's a genuine person in every respect. You can rely on what he says. We've had a few differences over the years, not many. Ian Millar is a first-class man of great talent, pride, and integrity.

Any criticism of Spruce Meadows is voiced primarily at the provincial level: available sponsorship money is inevitably drawn to Spruce Meadows, leaving smaller shows in Alberta, which might foster young riders, scrambling for backing. And competing at Spruce Meadows can be difficult. The 1989 prize lists, for example, feature sixty-four rules and regulations. Ron Southern has a fixation about cheating, which is admirable in a way, but he is unusually zealous in this regard. He told a riders' meeting at the start of the 1989 Masters competition that the show's corporate sponsors are his personal friends, and that if any rider was caught poling or drugging horses, he would dismantle Spruce Meadows and turn it into condominiums and a golf course.

Poling, or "rapping", is a training technique used to instil in the horse respect for jumps. Trainers on either side of a jump place a pole parallel to the jump and lift it as the horse goes over the rail, knocking the horse's legs. Convinced that he has to jump higher to clear the fence, the horse makes a bigger effort over succeeding jumps. Even though some trainers use it at home as a training technique, poling is considered cheating once the horse is stabled at a competition. Essentially, poling during the competition constitutes an unfair advantage.

There is a funny story told about a poling incident that apparently took place in Rotterdam a few years ago. A rider had spirited his horse out of the show area (which alone contravenes the rules) and had taken it to an adjoining park. The rider approached two men seated on a bench and asked them to move, because he planned to jump the bench while his aides poled the horse. Unfortunately for him, the two men on the bench were stewards at the competition. The rider was immediately ejected.

Medicating horses is another matter. I have absolutely no interest in performance-enhancing drugs. Aside from the obvious moral and ethical concerns, they do not work in the long-term, some of them could do terrible harm to the horse, and they could ruin my career. There are no easy or quick fixes in the riding and training of horses.

My position on the use of the commonly used anti-inflammatory Butazolidine (known as "Bute", and akin to Aspirin for humans) is this: at Millar Brooke we use the drug in a therapeutic way. If a horse has an ache from jumping on hard ground — and the footing can vary widely from show to show — or from a long haul on a truck, we might use the medication. Used properly, it is a healing agent that also makes the horse's job easier. But Lynn and I believe, extraordinary circumstances aside, that a lame horse should *not* compete if he is sound only by virtue of being on medication.

The problem in show jumping is that certain medications are allowed by some national equestrian federations and not by others. One competition, then, can be governed by two separate sets of drug rules. Riders can get into trouble by adhering to one set alone. My own case will illustrate the point.

In 1984 I was at Spruce Meadows with an inexperienced Big Ben. The horse was being given Banamine, an anti-inflammatory (like Aspirin, and certainly not performance-enhancing). The Canadian Equestrian Federation (CEF) allows its use; the international governing body (Fédération Equestre International, or FEI, one of the strictest federations) does not. Here is where it gets tricky: all Canadian national shows operate under CEF rules, with the exception of World Cup qualifiers, which make up a single class at these shows. Typically, the Spruce Meadows competition in 1984 was run under CEF drug rules, except for the World Cup qualifier, held Saturday under FEI rules.

The philosophical question becomes: if a forbidden medication that does not enhance performance is undetectable, does this make its use ethical? There is no right or wrong here, no black and white. If one federation approves a medication, does that mean the medication is appropriate? Or is the medication to be avoided altogether because another federation will not allow it?

What I do believe in is the correct veterinary treatment for these equine athletes. Treatment not only for sickness, but for sport injuries. The use of specific, prescribed medication must be carefully controlled and discontinued in time to clear the horse's system for testing purposes. If not, the rider not only breaks a rule but jeopardizes his reputation.

Regrettably, most people, including those inside the sport, do not distinguish between a positive drug test for a therapeutic medication and a positive drug test for a performance-enhancing substance. There is a world of difference. The first is an error in timing; the second is an attempt to take unfair advantage over one's competitors.

In this 1984 circumstance I decided to use the medication. It was particularly wet that year, so wet that some classes meant for the international ring were held in the drier national ring. I was concerned about the tremendous effort that Big Ben, a young horse, was having to make to jump out of the mud. Young horses can try too hard and become sore, mainly in their backs and hips. It was only Big Ben's second grand prix, and we were jumping him on a day-by-day basis. I spoke to a vet who suggested the anti-inflammatory Banamine, which has preventive value in that it limits soreness and is permitted under CEF rules; he further advised that if I planned to enter Big Ben in the World Cup qualifier, the medication must be stopped seventy-two hours prior to testing in order for it to clear the horse's system.

Big Ben did indeed compete in the qualifier, and won. Later he was tested and showed a trace of Banamine. We had stopped the medication seventy-two hours before the competition, so what had happened? There are three possible explanations. The medication was being administered orally in the horse's food. Big Ben is a notoriously slow eater, so it

is possible that a residue in his feed tub was not eaten until much later. Perhaps the explanation lay in the method used to administer the drug. Slower in, vets say, means slower out; a medication given orally to a horse leaves the system more slowly than one given intramuscularly, and slower even than one given intravenously. The third possibility, which I find unlikely, was sabotage.

There was an FEI hearing, to which I put my case in writing. They said it all sounded reasonable, fined me $1,000, and ordered that I return the prize money won in that event. Other riders, at Spruce Meadows and at other competitions, have occasionally been caught in that grey zone of

The mud on Big Ben's front feet shows it was a day of sloppy footing after heavy rains at Spruce Meadows.
(Andy Rose)

equine medication. Ron Southern, the riders know, takes an unforgiving view in this regard, but they respect him immensely. We all hope that no rider does anything in the future to render Spruce Meadows a haven for golfing or a site for condominiums.

We have brought four horses to Spruce Meadows — the stallions Winchester and El Futuro, the mare Pamino, and, of course, Big Ben. Strategy for these competitions begins in our kitchen at Millar Brooke Farm weeks beforehand. Lynn and I mull over which horses to bring, then marry the right horses with classes that suit their strengths. Since Air Canada no longer offers domestic horse transport, we truck the horses to all parts of Canada, first pairing them in twin stalls inside the van according to a carefully thought-out plan. Some horses, Lonesome Dove and Big Ben, for example, are great friends. Others make terrific enemies.

At Spruce Meadows, a groom's day starts about 5:00 A.M. and can go into the early evening — later if there are evening classes. Grooms are the backbone of the show-jumping world.

By 8:00 A.M. I am in the practice ring riding our horses, whether they compete this day or not, to keep them limber and mentally alert. We tailor the workout according to the tests we can expect to find in the ring. If the horse seems to lack confidence, we will lower the jumps in the practice ring; if he appears lazy, we'll raise them a bit.

For me, morning events in the All Canada ring (where national, as opposed to international events are held) can start as early as 9:00 A.M. Sometimes I'll have two horses in the same morning class, so that grooms Sandi Patterson and Christian Bordas are kept busy. Afternoon classes in the international ring may continue until 5:00 P.M. or 6:00 P.M.

Late in the day, before going back to the hotel, I do something that I consider important: I check on the horses. Do they have enough blankets, shavings for bedding? I will get a general feeling for the horses' moods and physical state, and, based on what I see, especially if I see fatigue, I will adjust the feed or maybe lighten up on the morning workout. I do this not to check up on my own people, who are among the best in the business, but because I feel it is necessary and because I desire that hands-on contact with our horses. Only then do I head back to my hotel.

The view of Calgary at night from Spruce Meadows is breathtaking. The air is crisp and clear. From these hills the city to the north looks like diamonds strewn on a black carpet. Sandi stays on the grounds, for she has an added responsibility: to keep Big Ben from harm. As the prize

An aerial view of a horse
jumping into the devil's
dyke at Spruce Meadows
(Andy Rose)

money grows, so does the temptation to sabotage a favourite, one worth
more than a million dollars. It would be easy to lace an apple or a dart
with a forbidden substance, leading to a long suspension for the rider.
The drug test is extraordinarily sensitive. A horse fed chocolate by a
child could turn a positive test for caffeine. Sabotage or careless-
ness: the result would be the same.

At the 1987 Royal Winter Fair in Toronto, a British rider was tagged
for giving his horse a banned substance. Over the years that horse had
won a lot, been tested a lot, but had never tested positive before. The
rider claimed sabotage and pointed the finger at the French team. He
managed to create enough doubt at the FEI hearing that they let him off.
The word "sabotage", then, has entered the language of our sport.

For that reason, Sandi, at Spruce Meadows anyway, sleeps on a cot in
the barn aisle by Big Ben's stall. She is a deterrent. Anyone wanting to get
at him in the middle of the night would have to step over her. It is not
common to take such precautions, but I will not be surprised if other
riders do the same in the days ahead.

The week for the Millar Brooke entries has gone well enough. There
have not been many victories, but we have been consistently in the
ribbons. On Wednesday, El Futuro turned in a clean round in the
Fletcher Challenge Cup, a speed class (one without a jump-off), but our
time was only good enough for sixth. Later the same day, Big Ben went
first and was flawless in an international class, but the time was not good
enough. Michael Whitaker, who has dominated the week-long competition, won the class on Mon Santa.

Winchester jumps an oxer with a liverpool at Spruce Meadows.
(Jayne Huddleston)

Thursday offered more of the same middling success. In a national open class (closed to international team horses), Pamino placed sixth and Winchester third in a jump-off. As the week continues, the purses have grown fatter: the idea is to have horse and rider peak when the big money is on the line. El Futuro seemed on schedule. We were fifth and clear in Thursday's international event. Late that day Big Ben went clear in the first round of a class, but caught a rail in the jump-off.

On Friday both Winchester and Pamino jumped off against two other horses in another national open class, and I found myself in the enviable position of having our two horses compete with each other for first and second prizes. El Futuro did not do well in Friday's international class, but we knew why. On Thursday he had driven a caulk (pronounced "cork", they are like cleats added to the horse's shoe to enhance footing) from one foot into his other front leg, just above the hoof. He seems a little sore, but I am confident of his toughness.

September 10, 1989. Today El Futuro showed us what he is made of. At noon, in an event called the Parcours de Chasse, we were up against a top international field. The Parcours is a speed class, the richest in the world, and normally a job for Winchester, who has lots of speed but not quite the scope of El Futuro. I put El Futuro — here to do the grand prix work if Big Ben ever got hurt — in this speed class to teach him something about speed, and he taught me something instead. He won, beating Mario Deslauriers on Box Car Willie by two-tenths of a second.

136

The victory tells me that El Futuro is a horse who will fight to overcome problems, such as a wet field. All winning horses have that quality. In eighty seconds, El Futuro has won $16,500. One night on Calgary television I watch the film *The Color of Money*. Paul Newman plays a pool shark, and his words sum up perfectly El Futuro's win: "Money won is twice as sweet as money earned."

But all this is so much preamble. Today at 1:45 P.M., on national television, thirty-seven riders are to compete in the du Maurier International for $526,000 in prize money. Just *finishing* the course will net a rider $2,000. John Whitaker was once asked if such mammoth purses change the otherwise friendly chemistry among riders, making them more serious. Just the opposite, he replied. Riders go to the other extreme to keep the pressure at bay. My own sense is that when the big money is on the line, riders do stay friendly, but they are more likely to withdraw into their own camps.

The du Maurier International consists of two rounds, the second round bringing back the top twelve riders over a shortened course, with a jump-off if necessary. Big Ben and I draw third position, not an enviable one, for it reduces the possibility of learning from the mistakes of others.

Before competing, riders — never horses — are permitted to walk the course. For the grand prix courses I do this twice, once in the morning after the designer has finished laying out the course, and once just before competing, so the course is fresh in my mind. A few years ago I was out walking a Spruce Meadows derby course, one that featured steep banks and other natural jumps. It had rained the night before, and I was checking the footing at the top of the bank when down I went — much to the amusement of the press corps and other riders. Spectators had yet to gather, so they missed out on my trip down the bank without my horse.

I spend more time walking the course than most other riders I know, and not just because I am concentrating on details of the course. I am safe out there, safe from journalists and spectators who might break my concentration. My main concern while walking the course is the distance between the jumps.

There are two ways of walking off the distance. One is to start at the bottom of the first jump and pace in three-foot strides to the bottom of the next jump. The rider then converts the total into horse strides, whose average length on course is twelve feet. So, a distance of sixty feet between jumps becomes five units of twelve or four horse strides, because we subtract one unit to allow for landing and take-off. Another way is to approximate the landing point of the horse — normally about six feet out from the jump — and then pace off horse strides to the estimated take-off spot for the next jump. I use both methods, since with certain jumps the horse will land at different spots.

Walking the course at Spruce Meadows with John Anderson of Calgary and Tom Gayford.
(Andy Rose)

137

As a test, course designers will create a distance between jumps that requires the horse either to shorten or lengthen his stride. The distance may call for a "quiet", or short, six strides, or a "forward", or long, five strides, or perhaps a "bending" six, if the line to a jump follows an arc. After walking the course, I have in my head a map of the course – which jump follows which, and the number and length of strides between jumps – as well as the shortened version of the course, should we make it to the jump-off.

While walking the course I also check on the rails and the footing; I imagine the course as the horse will see it; I conceive of ways to shave a second of time. I take notes: if hit by a horse's leg, that square rail will stay better than that round one; those rails are lighter than these and will fall more easily; and so on. Fences facing the in-gate are often troublesome because the horse may see the gate, think of heading to the barn, and lose concentration. The cups holding up planks may be flat; they may even be greased. Course designers are full of tricks. Courses today are equally a mental and a physical test for the horse. Horses learn by repetition, and those who have won the biggest titles in recent years are senior horses ten to fourteen years old. It takes a long time for them to be that good.

Course designers will present optical illusions for the horse: they will put, for example, a brightly coloured obstacle under a jump and blandly coloured rails on top. In the air, the horse drops his eye to look at the bright object, and then his balance is wrong. As in golf or tennis, where the eye looks is important, because it affects concentration and balance. After walking the course, I would anticipate that my horse might drop his eye at a particular jump, and take steps to prevent it: take a firmer hold of his mouth, apply a little more leg and seat, and sit deeper in the saddle on the approach to the jump.

My strategy for the du Maurier International is simple: two careful and clear rounds. Get to the jump-off. If Big Ben and I are to jump a course cleanly, then balance, pace, and take-off spot – it is a matter of inches – all have to be just right. The best riders are problem-solvers, so that when the plan they have created after walking the course comes unglued, they concoct a new one on the fly. I liken it to driving a car: approaching an intersection you see the light turn amber, and you must decide quickly whether to press the gas pedal or the brake. Both horse and rider need acute depth perception to make critical but snap judgements. How far away is the next fence? How many horse strides? Should I compress or lengthen the stride? It is called "having an eye", and all great riders have it. The eye measures the distance, the body senses the stride.

The planks are often tricky. Big Ben jumping at Spruce Meadows.
(Jayne Huddleston)

As I walk the course, designed by Jon Doney, I record its particular challenges:

1. The first vertical is a nice introductory jump. The flowers are tiered out in front, offering a bit of a ground line, which allows the horses to calculate the fence's height and helps them take off from the right spot. Normal cups on both ends and a normal rail.

2. As I pace the distance to the next jump — "the planks" (wide boards hung precariously on flat metal cups) — I note the normal seven-stride distance. The planks are big enough for a second jump, not as big as they would be if they came later in the course, but maybe that is a blessing. We are getting rid of the planks early in the course. On Saturday, the planks were later in the course and they caused a world of trouble.

3. Left turn to a yellow oxer (or spread fence). It is important to stay out to the right a little bit to get a straight line. But closer to the jump I notice the ground slopes off to the right and there is surface water on the

right side. So I will stay left a little. Lighter and with a smaller cup at one end, this rail will fall easily.

4. Again, I want to stay out a little because there is more than a ninety-degree turn to this next jump, another oxer. You do not want to get caught in angling across to this jump; you want to square up to it because it is big and wide. I note the light and very flat cup on the left side. This rail will not be forgiving.

5. I want to build up the pace a little bit for number five, the liverpool, or water jump. We jumped the water jump twice yesterday, and the horses get a little complacent if they jump it too many times. We will give it a real jump; that is a wide stretch of water.

6. No surprise that after jumping the big wide water we come to the skinny white vertical, as light as a feather. Again, unforgiving. The lightest rub would produce four faults. As to the distance, it is more a matter of breaking out, compressing the horse's stride, balancing him, getting him mentally under control. That is the most important ingredient in jumping that vertical, much more so than having any particular number of strides in mind.

7. Then on to the pair of liverpools. A normal twenty-four-foot one-stride. It is not the distance or size of these big oxers so much, more the distracting element of water underneath, which will make the horse drop his eye level and hence lead to balance and concentration problems.

8. On to a vertical, tall, away from the in-gate. Again, it will take a lot of organization. Neat right turn.

9. On to the big triple bar, which has a liverpool underneath it, and which requires a lot of power. Have to be careful with the triple bar, because of its flatness. It puts the horse out of shape to jump the next element, which includes a tight pair of verticals. That is the idea: to see which riders are educated to reshape their horses for the next test.

10. To the triple combination jump. Should be a quiet six strides to the vertical, then twenty-five feet to the next vertical, and twenty-four feet to the oxer. Requiring a lot of dexterity, the combination is a careful, stride-compressing exercise first, and then a power exercise to finish.

11. Around the corner. The time allowed will determine how tight a corner this will be. Number eleven is high and wide, coming late in the course, so a big test.

12. Finally, a steady, quiet five strides to the tall vertical. Overall, a good, world-class test in every way.

At 1:45, under skies that have finally cleared, we begin. The footing — which all week has been defeating both horses *and* riders — has improved under the warm sun and brisk winds. Big Ben and I go clear and stay well within the allotted ninety-eight seconds. But in round two the plan to go double-clear is dashed at the number-six fence, the skinny vertical I had been wary of, and the one that would haunt many riders this day. I ask Big Ben to sit back on his haunches for that jump, to reduce the possibility of his front feet hitting the rail. In effect, he overachieves and puts too *much* weight on his hind end at the point of take-off: he clears by six to eight inches in front, but catches a light rub behind. The rail bounces lightly, ponders staying in place, then lazily, almost in slow motion, falls.

Michael Whitaker on Mon Santa goes triple-clear and takes home the coveted show cooler and the cheque that goes with it. Big Ben and I settle for ninth, and a bonus for being top Canadian finisher.

There is no point in dwelling on downed rails. You simply learn from the mistake and you do not make it twice. I told the gathered press after the competition that the sport would drive you mad if you recorded every rail down and how much money each one costs you. I have been in the du Maurier too many times. In a heartbeat you can go, as Big Ben and I did in 1986 after knocking down the planks at the last jump, from second to twelfth.

One thing I do wonder about is the disadvantage of living and competing in Canada. European riders fly their horses to Calgary, and so get here relatively quickly. Canadian riders, on the other hand, have to transport their horses by trailer. Domestic air service, when it existed, was expensive, and only certain horses were flown. The rest went on the trucks. My own horses have spent fifty-seven hours in the trailer getting to Calgary. Ironically, I could have flown them to Amsterdam and then to Calgary in less time — and the horses would have been fresher at the other end. The cost, of course, would have been prohibitive.

September 11, 1989. My custom is to take the midnight flight out of Calgary Sunday night, so as not to lose a working day back home. After Spruce Meadows I draw up a balance sheet. The profit/loss statement comes down to expenses (horse transportation costs, entry fees, staff wages, and hotel bills) of $25,000, set against about $50,000 in prize money. I also tabulate another kind of balance sheet, looking back on my performance. Would I have done anything differently? Of course, I would not have knocked down that number-six fence. Spruce Meadows is a kind of stretching exercise. We are always up against quality.

Only back at Millar Brooke Farm do I let down a little. I see more clearly the stress and strain I had been under all week at one of the most demanding show-jumping tournaments in the world.

CHAPTER 9

The Hands-On Approach to High Finance

My mother and father wanted me to become a doctor or dentist, and though I never pursued a medical profession, I *do* know what it feels like to have a waiting room full of people who want to see me.

Let's go back to Spruce Meadows. At the end of a long day of exercising horses, competing in the ring, attending press conferences, and doing all the other things that comprise a day on the road, I head back to the barn on my motor scooter. (I had bought it for Lynn years ago, but I use it most.) In my red coat and black riding hat, and mounted on a scooter instead of Big Ben, I probably cut a ridiculous figure to anyone not used to the sight, but many riders have the scooters. They save a lot of time on show grounds as huge as Spruce Meadows.

Once at the barn I duck into the tack room. Not much larger than a walk-in closet, it serves all at once as equipment-storage-and-change room, makeshift office, and escape hatch. I call home on my cellular phone to talk to Lynn. How are she and Jonathon and Amy? All well with the other horses on the farm? What new developments on the business front?

Still on the phone, I emerge from the tack room wearing the black silk windbreaker given me by one of my corporate sponsors (Tod R. Rehm of Toshiba Information Systems Division), blue jeans, running shoes, and an Australian Snowy River hat whose tan colour is set off by a russet feather. I look and feel ready to relax. I am, in fact, on my way to the mini-Olympics, the Spruce Meadows tradition in which riders play games and unwind.

But there, seated on the Millar Brooke Farm tack trunk and standing by Big Ben's stall, are at least half a dozen people, all waiting to see me. The area has become a waiting room and the waiting room is full. There's Carol Kraushar of Centurion and Equi-Genesis, firms whose horse products I endorse. There are several owners of horses in the Millar Brooke stable. There's a journalist. There's Jayne Huddleston, the publisher of *Equesport Canada* magazine, here to report on the competition, but also under contract as my publicist. Where there is Jayne, journalists wanting interviews with Ian Millar are sure to follow. There is someone wanting my autograph. All these people represent important aspects of my sport and business, and many are close friends. I will somehow find time for them all.

At home I find myself in the same quandary: many demands on too little time. "Welcome to our insanity," I once told a first-time visitor to the farm. While I sometimes complain of the pace and the long line of people wanting to see me and talk to me, Lynn observes that I actually love the resulting flow of adrenalin. She accuses me of dallying before driving to an important dinner date or other occasion just so I can get my adrenalin moving, just so I have an excuse to speed. Perhaps it is true. I do love speed and adrenalin.

Also true is that, without all of our business concerns and attention to business, there would be no riding. I spend most of my time riding, training, and teaching, but "doing business" is also clearly a priority. I mean by that term an ongoing sensitivity to business concerns and the instinct that tells me when to push hard in a transaction and when to relent. Some horsemen and horsewomen, rigid in their dealings, can antagonize business associates, and in the long term they lose — both in business and in riding. I never forget that the two are intertwined.

If I am to compete with the best, high-quality (and therefore expensive) horses are essential. A rider without private funding had better learn to interest investors, attract corporate sponsors, and acquire

I am wearing my black Toshiba windbreaker for this interview in Sweden with Ted Reynolds of CBC-TV.
(Jayne Huddleston)

business acumen, because show jumping is one expensive and complicated sport. I have an adding machine on my desk at Millar Brooke Farm for a reason.

The enemy is overhead. It can take up to a million dollars just to begin to fight the grand prix fight. The minimum initial outlay looks like this:

1. Barn with twenty-five stalls — $75,000
2. Arena for all-weather training — $125,000
3. Miscellaneous horse equipment — $25,000
4. Horse trailers and trucks — $75,000
5. Set of jumps — $15,000
6. Fencing — $25,000
7. Footing for outdoor ring — $10,000
8. Storage barn — $20,000
9. Farm equipment, tractors, etc. — $20,000

All this approaches $400,000, before tallying the cost of land, working capital, and the horses themselves. Horse bills can add up quickly: feed and board, entry fees at shows, insurance, plane trips, veterinary care, blacksmiths' fees, grooms' wages. Even a younger horse with only limited travel expenses can incur an annual maintenance bill of $35,000 to $40,000; a grand prix horse, one on the ten-month North American and European circuit, can cost $50,000 to $60,000 a year to maintain and show in the ring. Since we sometimes have twenty-four horses in our stables, half a dozen of them grand prix and speed horses, the total bill can add up to a staggering figure.

The money to sustain such an operation comes from several sources, and all are important. I rank them below, in the order of their importance to our operation.

Owners and investors: My most important sponsors, owners of horses and investors in syndicates (I will explain that term shortly) also participate in the costs of developing young horses. During the first few years, owners and investors face huge maintenance costs with little or no prize money coming in. If a preliminary (or first-year) horse wins $5,000 to $7,500 in a year he has done exceptionally well; an intermediate horse who wins $10,000 in a year has also done well. In general, a senior horse, a grand prix horse, should pay his own way. He should win at least as much money as it costs to keep him. In many cases, owners and investors are billed by the rider for maintenance costs — an important source of support.

Corporate support: This is an increasingly important means of backing. In exchange for discreetly displaying a corporate name or logo on a saddle pad, along with a commitment to spend a certain number of days per year at speaking engagements, press conferences, and corporate functions, the amateur rider earns some financial support from a firm. I have that sort of arrangement with both Toshiba Information Systems Division and the Bank of Montreal.

Riders can endorse company products as part of advertising and promotion. My own list includes Centurion, an electro-magnetic machine used in physiotherapy for horses, and that same company's feed supplement line called Equi-Genesis Products; a saddle, called the Vision Saddle, that I developed with Paul Morgan, a tack-shop owner in Ottawa, which is distributed by Miller's Saddlery of New York, the largest wholesaler of horse products in the world; a line of hats — my Snowy River hat, for example — and rain gear called Koolah; and Frantisi,

Bill Mulholland of the Bank of Montreal poses with Big Ben during a press reception to announce the signing of our sponsorship contract.
(Jayne Huddleston)

distributors of a line of riding clothes, some of which I endorse. All of these endorsements are three-way contracts, involving the firm, myself, and the Canadian Equestrian Federation (CEF). The money is directed to me through the CEF so as not to jeopardize my amateur status. The CEF holds the money in trust, and advances funds to cover my competition-related expenses.

Prize money: Naturally, this is a hard one to budget for, but if all goes well, it should be a rider's major source of income. Big Ben alone, for example, wins on average $125,000 to $150,000 a year, but he has won more. In 1987 he won $200,000. He is, however, unusual. Most grand prix horses win, on average, approximately $50,000 a year.

Teaching: Teaching also brings in money, although I no longer conduct the eight or ten three-day clinics a year I did in the past. My hectic competition schedule will not allow it.

Horse dealing: Riders who are also trainers of horses (and most are) can earn money buying and selling their own horses, and can gain commission income from doing the same for others.

Government support: As a member of the Canadian equestrian team (CET) and as an international Sport Canada "carded" athlete, I am entitled to a monthly living allowance, which is sent to me through Sport Canada. The CET also offers travel assistance to certain international events and a hotel subsidy when a rider is representing Canada.

The list of ways to keep money coming into Millar Brooke is long, but it has to be; the list of expenses is equally long. For the same reason the

Public speaking is one of the things that I am called upon to do on behalf of my corporate sponsors.
(Howard Rosenberg)

rider, unless of independent means, must possess business savvy. Unlike the hockey player, by comparison, who need not worry about hotel reservations and ticket sales or whether the rink is unlocked and the team doctor is there, the rider organizes every facet of his sport.

I am not sure this makes us better athletes, but it certainly keeps life interesting. When I rode at Dwyer Hill in the 1970s, my job was mainly riding. I had certain managerial functions, and did some book-keeping, and I must admit, there were times when I was under-challenged. I felt insulated from reality. Any entrepreneur gains satisfaction from making the business work. That was missing at Dwyer Hill. Since 1980, when Lynn and I started Millar Brooke, I have *never* felt under-challenged. The trick in balancing business and show jumping is to keep the focus on riding and training. When I am working with a horse, that is *my* time with him. I will not allow interruption then.

But business does occupy one-third of my time at home and probably one-fifth of my time on the road. My entire approach to the business aspect of riding is a hands-on one. Like anyone managing a small business, I had better know on a thirty-day basis where I stand with payables and receivables.

The costs can run up fast on the road. I can look at a credit-card record and know — depending on where we were competing — if the amounts are correct. I am often rewarded by my diligence. Once I found that two grooms had paid the same hotel bill. I am not God's gift to accounting, but where my money is being spent, I tend to be thorough. Typically, I do the bank deposits myself. Experience has taught me the importance of such attention to detail.

On the other hand, an extreme hands-on approach has its own pitfalls. I collect bits of wisdom wherever I can find them, and for years I had pinned on my office wall a phrase that touched on the danger of *not* delegating. I had found it in an airline magazine, and it went something like, "Don't ask who could do this job the best, ask who *should* be doing this job." There is a danger in thinking that you can do jobs better than anyone else and deciding to do them all; you may bottleneck an entire operation.

As a compromise between two extremes, I have learned to delegate certain responsibilities. I now know which ones I am wiser to delegate and which I had better handle myself. It would be easy for me to fix my attention on riding and teaching, while delegating finance, but that would be a mistake. Some horsemen learn this lesson the hard way.

A good friend of ours in North Carolina (we bought Warrior and Brother Sam from him) had employed a business manager to handle all financial operations on the farm. One day, the manager decided to leave

Big Ben in the jump-off for the $80,000 Chrysler Derby at Spruce Meadows
(Jayne Huddleston)

town, and she took all his money with her. She pocketed every cent that horseman had. A similar calamity unfolded at Dwyer Hill when a business manager took advantage. This much I learned from my early days with my business partner John Rivington, while acquiring and losing a fortune in the real-estate, hotel, and restaurant business: you have to be in control, especially in a small business.

At Millar Brooke I also have to know how each horse is contributing or not contributing to the enterprise. For that reason, each horse has a file that will tell me at a glance how and when expenses were incurred, including blacksmith and veterinary work; prize money and how and when it was won are similarly recorded. This system evolved in the first several years while I was doing all record-keeping myself. With twelve monthly statements, I had a complete picture of each horse for that year.

In 1983, Roger St. Jacques (an Ottawa businessman whose daughter I was teaching), my partner Eve Mainwaring, Fritz and Lilian Bollinger, and Lynn and I conceived of a strategy to encourage investment in show-jumping horses. Syndication, as it came to be known, creates an association whose investment rises and falls with the fortunes of horses in that syndicate. Unique in show jumping, although fairly common in thoroughbred racing, it has been very successful for us.

The four of us pooled three horses, three proven grand prix horses (Big Ben, Warrior, and Wotan), that combinations of us jointly owned. We formed a company, Canadian Show Jumpers Unlimited Inc., then sold the horses — which we valued at $200,000 each — to the company in exchange for shares in the company and promissory notes for the balance. We then set about selling twenty shares, at $30,000 each, until all of us were paid back.

Under the terms of the contract, Millar Brooke Farm agreed to manage and handle the training and showing of these three horses. The farm also agreed to absorb the loss if a shortfall occurred (if expenses exceeded prize money). However, in its five-year existence the company has made a profit every year. Warrior and Wotan have since been sold, but the company now owns outright one promising young horse, Canadian Colours, along with shares in another, Domingo; and of course we own 100 per cent of Big Ben. I also channel a percentage of my corporate sponsorship income to the company.

Canadian Show Jumpers Unlimited is a particular type of syndicate. Each of four separate syndicates operates according to the wishes of those who create it and participate in it.

But to make syndicates work, I do indeed have to put my money where my mouth is. Potential investors want to see that riders have their own money invested. They want to feel that I am committed, that I will leave no stone unturned to make these horses successful. They are not wrong in that assumption. Many other riders simply will not, or cannot, invest their own money in a horse.

Syndication does not exist anywhere else in the world in the way that Lynn and I have established it. The key to our type of syndication is that we sell the steak, never the sizzle: I never promise or guarantee success. That's selling the sizzle. Many riders and trainers, trying to entice investors, paint an unrealistic and inflated picture of the horse as an investment, and if things turn sour, the investors can feel taken advantage of.

What I say to potential investors, if the syndicate has been built around a promising young horse, is that we have two years of expenses to put into him, so there will be heavy development costs, with little income, over a two-year period. If the horse works out, by the third year prize money should cover, or even exceed, expenses. In his fourth year, he should definitely show a profit. He might be worth $200,000, possibly $1 million. If he does not become a grand prix horse, but learns well, he might become a "second" horse, specializing in speed classes, and be worth $250,000. Or he could become a good amateur horse, worth $75,000 to $200,000. He could, of course, get hurt and be worth nothing. And statistics would suggest that the chance of him becoming a million-dollar grand prix horse is slim.

Wotan jumping at Spruce Meadows
(Jayne Huddleston)

One of many red ribbons for Warrior at Spruce Meadows
(Jayne Huddleston)

Investors get involved for financial reasons, of course, but for many other reasons too. Maybe they simply like horses. They may invest for fun, to feel involved in the sport, to support the Canadian equestrian team. But return on investment is not the only reason, and a good thing too, for there are no sure things in show jumping. I would never want an erstwhile investor to lament, "Oh, that horse deal. Never again." I want potential investors to know the unvarnished truth: about 98 per cent of all horses starting off on the road to the grand prix ring never make it there. I lose investors by saying that, but if they come on board, they know the score first. We keep them informed and involved. I put together a regular newsletter, and when I am on the road, I call back to Paula with results, which she passes along.

Keeping investors informed and feeling involved is an art in itself, requiring that the horseman be people-smart as well as horse-smart. When I was a boy trying to make money to ride horses by selling newspapers or magazine subscriptions, I was a hard-sell expert. It did not matter if my potential buyers had triple pneumonia or had just declared bankruptcy; I would corner them, and they bought because I won them over or because it was the only way to get rid of me. Over time, I have learned a great deal about people by working with horses. Horses taught me subtlety and timing.

Showing the crowd a cheque earned in the lucrative Chrysler Derby at Spruce Meadows
(Jayne Huddleston)

A network of financial support has evolved at Millar Brooke, and it now includes four separate syndicates and a host of individual backers, some fifty-five or sixty groups or individuals in all. Our backers tell us that they admire the business-like atmosphere at Millar Brooke. Our method of operation is effective, and quite a change from the farm's early days, when we had little support and spread ourselves rather thin. At that time we were developing hunters, teaching riders, breaking horses, competing – doing everything. We were like a cork going down the river. Where the river went, the cork went. Somewhere along the line we saw a need for control.

Two unrelated influences helped us to become specialists and to establish new priorities. One year a corporate sponsor became involved with the American equestrian team. The sponsor produced a motivational film and advised the team that, while they could do a lot of things, they should stick to what they do better than anyone else. The second nudge came from George Morris, who once told me, "Never be afraid to create a void. You never know what will fill it." He meant that Lynn and I should have confidence, that the void – if we created one – would be filled in a meaningful way.

At Millar Brooke, then, we specialized. We created a void, and we established new priorities: I would be a rider and trainer first, a teacher of riders second, and a buyer and seller of horses third. Someone else could do all those other things.

But even that radical shift did not change the basic workings of Millar Brooke Farm. If there are to be not one but two *o*'s in Millar Brooke (a tired joke, but I still use it), and if our success is to continue, every member of the team has to pull his or her weight. Posted on a wall in our barn is a graphic illustration of the saying, "You are only as strong as your weakest link." A drawing depicts seven links of a chain, and in the middle is a first-prize ribbon from the 1987 Spruce Meadows National Tournament. The seven links have names: owner, blacksmith, veterinarian, groom, horse, trainer, rider.

If I ever began to slip in the grand prix standings, if over time our horses became injury-prone, or if our backers gradually moved on, I would re-examine that chain and see where the problem lay. Are grooms missing signs that would have spared a horse a career-threatening injury? Are we neglecting owners? Am I spending too little time on the horses? My friend Roger St. Jacques, a business consultant, says to his clients about their troubled businesses, "I may not tell you anything that you don't already know about your business, but I will remind you to do things you used to do but for some reason stopped doing." Take care of the basics in the operation, and none of these problems will occur.

When I was a boy I never wanted to go to bed. I was afraid I would miss something. Even today, if I do not ride those horses every day, I fear some little thing will be missed. I am driven to be thorough. I always want to reduce the risk of things going wrong. My success, I am convinced, is vulnerable. The Canadian horseman Robert Meilsoe, who lives in Schomberg, Ontario, once observed that, "Ian Millar's particular form of paranoia is a reality-based fear: Ian's always afraid that someone else got up an hour ahead of him or trained an hour more."

For me and for the staff at Millar Brooke Farm, teamwork pays off — literally. Five per cent of the prize money earned by our horses is dispersed among staff. Grooms at competitions earn bonuses if a horse records a major victory. Excellence is its own reward, but human nature being what it is, a little encouragement also helps.

We get that encouragement in more than just financial ways. In 1987, *L'Année Hippique*, the prestigious yearbook of international equestrian sports, ranked me at the top in its show-jumping ratings. This is, in effect, the rider-of-the-year award. In 1988, Big Ben and I slipped to third, but in 1989 we were back on top. The yearbook's editor, a Swiss writer named Max E. Ammann, annually gathers data, reports, and photos in a large hardbound volume of over five hundred pages. In show jumping he looks at results from major international competitions, Nations' Cup, and grand prix events. I consider the ranking a great honour, but it is absolutely true that the Millar Brooke team — all those people who make up the chain — is the real winner: Claude Bollinger shipping the horses so carefully on the long hauls; Lynn maintaining the horses, etc. "Success comes from working together" was a phrase I uttered during a casual conversation with the producer of a series of commercials I did with the Bank of Montreal. He was on it like a hen on a June bug; it was used in the commercials, and it truly captures the essence of Millar Brooke Farm.

A few truths should by now be clear about show jumping and the part I play in it. One, I am a partner — with horses, owners, trainers, grooms, vets, and blacksmiths. And two, the horse business is indeed a *business*, with its own hopes and fears: hopes for profit, fears of losses.

But I am also an entrepreneur engaged in business that has nothing to do with horses specifically; although in the long run it has everything to do with horses. If I am to play the horse game and participate as an owner, I have to play the money game. If I succeed in the money game, I keep on playing the horse game, and along the way I put aside what amounts to a pension for Lynn and me and some security for Amy and Jonathon. In both games, partners and luck are recurring themes. In both, I trust my instincts, and if I trust the person I am dealing with, I tend to trust that the deal will be a good one.

A story will illustrate my point about both partnership and luck. When I was still a stockbroker, John Woods was director of finance for the Liberal Party of Canada. He was involved in a certain penny stock, Lynx Canada Explorations. Every time Lynn and I had any money, we put it in Lynx. Whenever my clients asked me for a tip, I would say, "Well, actually, I'm pretty high on this Lynx Canada."

My manager, Vic Wilgress, kept seeing Lynx coming up on the accounts, and one day he called me into his office.

"Ian," he said, "I'm not saying anything bad about John, but penny mines? They told you about this on your course. A high percentage of these ventures fail."

"Not this one," I said. "Besides, John was my best man. I believe in him totally."

Lynx had a delayed opening on the stock exchange. We had bought the stock when it was valued at between 24¢ and 60¢. Finally the big day came. It opened at about $2, banged around at $2.10, $2.15. It was going wild. Everybody was beside themselves with excitement.

"Into my office," said Vic. I liked him. Ex-Navy. He was standing behind his desk, and looking at me. "You get that Lynx off your books now."

With Jason Cheon, the Korean rider who bought Warrior
(Andy Rose)

"But Vic — "

"Now!"

"But Vic. John said — "

"I don't want to hear what John said. I'm telling you. Get it off your books now."

So, out I went. I got on the phone and advised all my clients to bail out. I sold every share we owned too, at $1.95 to $2.10. You can still find Lynx on the stock exchange today. Last time I looked it was sitting at around 24¢.

We had done it: bought low, sold high, made a killing — allowing us to buy the farm at Perth. But I could have lost it all if Vic had not been there to ram down my throat the decision to sell. The stock was in its distribution phase. My belief in John got me into the deal; luck and Vic got me out with a significant profit.

Flush with that success, I formed a partnership with John Rivington, a classmate and bridge partner from my college days. John and I would learn some hard lessons, but we never lost faith in our partnership.

We had both studied business administration. He was eight years older than me. We both came from farms and were the only two who drove half-ton trucks to school. He was entering the world of real estate, interest rates were low, and he was about as crazy and aggressive as I was. Inspired by someone who had written a book about how to make millions in real estate, we began. In about a year, and with approximately $50,000 of real money, we owned about $1 million in real estate in the Ottawa area.

John and I were buying everything from duplexes to four-unit apartment buildings and rooming houses near Ottawa University. Then we decided we needed more cash flow, because all the rents were used to cover the interest and mortgage payments, leaving nothing for us to live on. We had an idea. In those days, there were submarine shops, pizza shops, and char-broiled hamburger shops. But nobody had put them under one roof. We would go out into the country and do just that. We bought a little grocery store right on Highway 7 in Perth, and we converted it to the first Minute Man restaurant. We set up another one in Arnprior. Then we bought a hotel in Sharbot Lake. John and I were like a train, and it was always full steam ahead. By this time the stock brokerage and CBC jobs were on the shelf. I had fallen in love with Perth, and Lynn and I had closed the deal on the farm in 1972.

Suddenly the wheels fell off. Climbing interest rates had us in a cash-flow bind and facing bankruptcy by early 1973. However, neither of us wanted to declare bankruptcy. We therefore began selling every piece of property, and over time we repaid every nickel of the staggering debt that each of us had accumulated. We both remember what a difficult,

Canadian Colours, one of the young horses in the Millar Brooke stable, jumping
(Jayne Huddleston)

even devastating time this was. We came out with nothing but a lot of eighteen-hour days behind us and a tremendous education. Broke but wiser. That experience put a large measure of financial caution into both our lives.

These days our firm, Jebb's Creek Investments (named after a creek that crosses the Millar Brooke Farm property), is very much in the black. I read once that "A rich man is one who knows when he has enough." I suppose I am not rich. John has since become a real-estate appraiser and does very well in that business. Together, we have bought an entire block in the town of Smiths Falls. I have another real-estate partnership with a Perth car-dealer named Ken Dick. And so we play the game. I do so because my sport requires it. But the thrill of the game is in many ways its own reward. I like the mental challenge, the diversion, the sense of release it gives me.

At Millar Brooke I tend to ride herd on every penny. John does the same with Jebb's Creek Investments. But as partners in our real-estate dealings, John and I are more inclined to step back and look at the overall picture. He is my partner and next to Lynn, my closest friend. We never disagree and only move when both of us are sure; we have complete trust in one another.

Wise partnerships — with Lynn or with John or with the horses themselves — have always been at the heart of my success. In picking the right partners, I have been truly fortunate.

CHAPTER 10

Training Horses: 'Water on Stone'

The old one-room schoolhouses were arranged so that one teacher could cope with all eight grades. Often there were eight rows, each row consisting of pupils in a particular grade. Row 1 was Grade 1, Row 2 was Grade 2, and so on to Grade 8. We wonder today how teachers managed to instruct younger and older pupils and all those in between.

Big Ben enjoys the freedom of his paddock at Millar Brooke Farm.
(Jayne Huddleston)

A rider who also trains horses — and that would describe me — does much the same thing. The only difference is that our students can range from Grade 1 all the way to post-graduate university. At any one time Millar Brooke stables some twenty horses. There are the post-grad students, such as Big Ben and Winchester; the bright ones in university, such as El Futuro and Lonesome Dove; and the very young ones, barely out of kindergarten, who show promise as they learn elementary aspects of show jumping. Like a teacher in a one-room schoolhouse, I know their personalities and scholastic records, but my method is more instinctive and impressionistic than purely structured. In almost everything I do, instinct precedes analysis.

Every day is school day. Every day the teacher himself learns something new from his charges. Some days they come to the schoolyard spoiling for a fight; some days they come insisting that two and two make five. Some days they are entirely cooperative. But for me, school is always an exhilarating place to be.

I love working with young horses. The process is very special, full of rewards. Like an explorer, I never know where my exploration might take me. There is always the chance that this one, or maybe that one, will be another Big Ben.

When I begin to train a horse, I am essentially selling him something — the skills required to be a grand prix jumper. Selling, whether to horses or humans, requires a certain knack. I have often felt that Fuller Brush sales people would have made eminent horse trainers. Their method of selling to humans is not unlike my own method of selling to horses. Imagine this scene: a home-owner or apartment-dweller comes to the door in the morning, in no mood for a salesman. The place is a disaster.

The seller's first job is to encourage and elicit the "yes" response. "My, what a beautiful house!" he says, quite oblivious to the chaos all around. "Who was your interior decorator?"

The would-be buyer looks at him as if he is mad, but listens anyway. The seller notices a wedding picture somewhere inside the rubble and wonders aloud if the person standing there is newly wed, when clearly that is not the case. He creates a mood to elicit the right response, knowing that it is easier to sell brushes if the right mood is established. The same principle applies to horses. In the beginning I ask them to perform relatively inconsequential deeds. That way I am more likely to get the "yes" response to more sophisticated requests later on with minimum resistance. I always follow up with as much of a reward as I think the animal deserves, to add encouragement and confidence.

With any horse I train, I have to take control. Good jumpers are by nature brave and aggressive, but the steam-roller approach to training only compromises the mysterious X-factor that could have spawned greatness. Greatness comes from the heart and the head. If the horse's training is overly structured and he is overly intimidated, he may become a well-trained jumper, but some of his spark, some of his spirit is lost. His individuality is sacred and must be left to him.

The story of Winchester, a black Hanoverian stallion, is a case in point. Sent to me as a four-year-old by his owners, he was as talented a young horse as I had ever seen. A brilliant athlete, a brilliant jumper.

He was also tough, too tough. The first time I saw him it took three people to catch him in the stall to tack him up. He was wild. I got on him, and he gave me a ride! It took three hours of riding him merely to gain control. For most of the three hours, I had no idea who was going to win. The next day it took an hour and a half. From that point forward, he was my horse. If someone else was handling him and having trouble, all the horse had to do was hear my voice, and he would cooperate. I did not terrorize him. He simply gained a respect for me, and I for him. The relationship was solid.

He was coming along nicely when his owners became embroiled in an extended quarantine after buying some horses in Europe. As a result all their horses — including Winchester — were taken back to their farm. The owners intended to return Winchester to me, but later decided against it and found him another rider. The combination did not work. The stallion refused to go around the courses. He would stop, rear, and spin. Winchester and that rider parted company. Next, a European rider tried his hand. Again no success. By this time Winchester was five years old. Although he was eventually used as a dressage and later as a breeding horse, none of that early promise was met.

Finally, when Winchester was nine or ten years old, the owners encountered financial difficulties. At an ensuing auction, Eve Mainwaring, my partner in many a horse deal, hoped to buy Winchester — but for no more than $20,000. We asked a veterinarian to examine him, but he stopped partway through the examination. The horse had been badly treated, and the vet advised against buying him. Eve bid anyway, higher than we wanted to go (she never did say how high), but not high enough. An American woman named Laura Thorn bought him, because she liked his blood lines and breeding, but mostly because she felt sorry for him. All of the horses from this farm were in tough shape.

One day I received a call from the new owner. By then Winchester was stabled at her Thornbrook Farm outside New York City. She had heard about my early success with Winchester; the vets at Cornell University had taken a long look at him and they believed he could be rehabilitated. Would I come down to her farm and talk about all of this? I did. I rode the horse for the first time in five or six years, and it was like yesterday: the chemistry was unbelievable and instantaneous. I was convinced he remembered me. I jumped him over some fairly big jumps, and he responded terrifically. Laura and I agreed that Winchester would return to Millar Brooke to see if he might have a show-jumping career after all.

At home Winchester was still tough, but somewhere along the line that fight had been taken out of him. To say that his spirit was broken sounds like something from a Walt Disney animal film, but something was missing from the horse.

We have had him since May of 1987, and what an extraordinary acquisition he has been. Backing up Big Ben and El Futuro in the international division time and time again, he has an enviable record. He won, for example, the Loblaws Classic World Cup Qualifier at Sunnybrook Park in the summer of 1989. But had I not known the horse as a four-year-old, I would not know that a future among the top echelons of grand prix horses had been denied him.

A top-of-the-line horse is a fighter. As a trainer, my objective is to channel the fight to work for me, and *against* the jumps and the mountain I want him to climb. By training, by orchestrating his attitude, motivation, and concentration, I establish a partnership with him. He comes to know that his partner will help him overcome problems in the ring. Every time I ride that horse, I am telling him that I believe in him. Every time we compete, I am telling him that I believe in our ability to perform miracles.

Winchester is a top international horse. International riders bring two horses to big events: their grand prix horse (often Big Ben in my case), and a "second" horse (often Winchester), specializing in speed and novelty classes. Terribly important to a rider, a top second horse competes in more classes, does more work, and in many ways has to be more versatile. Winchester's story is truly wonderful, because he defies all odds in being as good as he is. Only thirteen years old and very fast, he may jump a long time, because during all those early years he did not jump at all. The tragedy is that Winchester could perhaps have been a grand prix horse of Big Ben's stature.

As a trainer, then, I want to establish control, but not at the expense of the horse's spirit, that spark at the heart of greatness.

Also terribly important in the training of a horse are the basics, what horse aficionados call "flatwork" — transitions into and out of the walk, trot, and canter, circles, canter-lead changes, the lengthening and shortening of strides, or "stride control" — all the essential skills that a show jumper has to learn before even looking at a fence to jump. I am on a horse at 8:30 most mornings of my life, teaching slowly and patiently just such basics. The minute I think these little things do not matter any

Winchester, the hard-luck horse who has accomplished so much, at a tournament in Ottawa.
(Jayne Huddleston)

more, I redouble the effort. I only jump the horses a few times a week if I am at home; but five and six times a week they get flatwork.

Stride control is as important to my sport as practising scales on a piano is to a pianist. It is the ability of a horse to open and close his stride as necessary. Early on in Big Ben's career it was one of the hardest things to teach him, even though he is a horse who learns faster than any horse I have ever trained. He has a big powerful stride. If the average horse covers a certain distance between jumps in nine strides, Big Ben comfortably covers the same distance in seven. But the stride that comes most naturally to a horse is not always the ideal one. Horses usually find it easy to lengthen their strides, more difficult to compress. Both are important. The horse has to shorten and lengthen his stride while maintaining his balance.

Think of a horse cantering along and you, the rider, have lengthened his stride. If you had been using a metronome to measure out his canter stride, the lengthened stride should still conform to the beat. In other words, the stride lengthens, it does not quicken. Similarly, if the horse shortens his stride, the rhythm of the stride should not slow.

Stride control is taught during flatwork. Once the horse has mastered the skill on the flat, I introduce it in his jumping work. One technique is to employ cavaletti, poles six feet long set varying distances apart, either on the ground or just off the ground. As the horse trots over cavaletti set on the ground or canters in different stride lengths over higher cavaletti, he is learning another lesson too: he is developing an "eye". Sounds simple, but a horse has to worry about both his front end and his hind end. In human terms, it could be likened to that physical trick you probably did as a child, patting your head and rubbing your stomach at the same time. It takes practice.

Lessons learned on the cavaletti transfer quite well to gymnastic exercises. These involve a series of small jumps never more than three strides apart and rarely exceeding three feet, six inches high. Essentially, gymnastics teach the horse to apply all of the skills he has learned in his flatwork. They also teach him to use his power and technique and to refine them both. Mentally, they teach him to be patient, to study the jumps — not to rush or attack them — and to use his skills to solve the problems posed by the gymnastic exercises. At Millar Brooke, Lynn and I use gymnastics much more than most trainers. We have devised at least a dozen progressively more difficult gymnastic layouts. The horse may take several months to master all of them, but I am a purist in the training department, so I prefer not to put a time frame on how long all this might take. We advance to the next level when the horse is ready. But even after that I will continue to use gymnastics to keep the horses supple and conditioned, and to review basic jumping skills.

Lynn, a trainer whose judgement I trust, is protective of the young horses in the Millar Brooke stable. She calls them her "babies", and I tease her sometimes by telling her that while she was in Perth on an errand, I schooled one of her babies over a bigger jump than she would have approved.

Training a horse is like making dessert. The cake comes first, long before you put on the icing. There are people in the equestrian world who do nothing *but* bake cakes (turn out horses trained in the basics), leaving others to put on the grand prix icing. But I need to know that the cake was baked just right, and I have had better luck (while saving money) doing it myself. I may have to spend four years turning a green four-year-old horse into a grand prix jumper — with no guarantee of that ever happening — but I relish the challenge. To continue my metaphor, I love baking a cake and putting the icing on myself.

Meeting a young foal from the breeding program at Spruce Meadows
(Jack Cusano/*Calgary Sun*)

For that reason I prefer warm-blooded horses. When horsemen and horsewomen talk about warm- , cold- , and hot-blooded horses, they refer more to the horse's disposition than to its breeding. When I was a young rider, the horses I learned to compete on and who in turn taught me, were hot-blooded, sensitive, and sometimes high-strung thoroughbreds. Cold-blooded horses are quieter and less responsive; they lack competitive zeal. Warm-bloods stand somewhere between the two extremes. A warm-blooded horse, such as Big Ben, has a disposition: a unique temperament, an inclination, a mind of his own. I am more comfortable working with warm- and hot-blooded horses, what I call "blood horses". Their minds interest me, and in my experience a blood horse will come through for a rider where a cold-blooded horse may not.

I remember a study conducted on domestic animals to determine their powers of reasoning. The pig ranked high, the horse lower. But the horse, it turned out, was shown to have great ability to learn by rote, and to remember his lessons. Unlike a student who crams in April and has forgotten by September, a horse remembers. The trick is to teach him the right things and never allow him to reach the wrong conclusion.

Other studies have suggested that horses cannot reason, but I am less certain. When we were in Indianapolis for the Pan-American Games in 1987 and Big Ben had the abscess in his foot, we wanted him to stay on a rubber mat while we tried to lift his hoof. We would not have attempted that procedure on the cement floor — only on the mat — for fear of him falling. The mat offered secure footing, the cement did not. Big Ben somehow knew that he was safe from our meddling when he was on the concrete. How had he come to that conclusion? I do not overestimate a horse's intelligence, but neither do I underestimate it.

Horse training is a delicate art. Essentially, you are dealing with a big, strong adolescent. You want to gain control, but if the whole business becomes too confrontational, the horse will only remember the brawl, and not the lesson that provoked the brawl. As a trainer, then, I am more of a repeater. I work like water dripping on a stone. I avoid escalation whenever possible.

I learned from Dr. Bode when I was a boy that patience is the key. He knew that a horse would learn when the horse was ready to learn. Knowing *when* — and I think this lesson applies in life too — is just as important as *how*.

Here is another pillar in the system I employ in training a horse: I believe that the communication between horse and rider must be subtle. I want to teach the horse sensitivity, so that he listens to my whispers, and I never have to resort to shouting. In training and in competition, I always start by *asking* the horse to do something. If that fails, I *tell* him to do it. The final step is to *demand* that he do it, but I never want to reach that stage. *Ask. Tell. Demand.*

Let me illustrate with an example of what transpires in the show ring between horse and rider. Since I will use the word *balance* often, the reader should understand what I mean by the term.

We talk in show jumping about the need for a rider to be "in balance"; the horse must be too. A horse without a rider will naturally carry about 60 per cent of his body weight on the front end, 40 per cent on the hind end. The horse is thus naturally "on his forehand". We say the horse is "collected" when the rider gets him to transfer weight from the front end to the back end and the hind end comes in underneath his barrel. The height of his hindquarters even lowers a bit. While galloping to a jump, we want the horse balanced so that he carries 50 per cent of his weight on his hind end and the other 50 per cent on his front end. In some cases, the rider might ask for a more extreme weight distribution — up to 60 per cent on the hind end.

Now, let us enter the ring. Here my aim is to influence the horse's balance, power, length of stride, and concentration in order to accomplish a clean and/or fast round, as the case may be. In one sense I am

*Big Ben going over one of
the unique jumps at Seoul*
(Jayne Huddleston)

initiating action: I am saying to the horse, "Here's where I'd like you to go, and here's the speed and balance, here's the length of stride, etc." But I am also constantly reacting to how the horse responds to the jumps, footing, and factors outside the ring (tents, umbrellas, stands, people, trucks, noises). When I first ride into the ring, I normally have fifteen to twenty seconds before the audible tone sounds to signal the start of the round, and sixty seconds after it sounds, I must have reached the first jump. I will have selected beforehand a certain area of the ring or set of jumps that I want the horse to see in that time. I will therefore ride in that area before starting on course. During that first minute in the ring I want 70 per cent of his concentration; he may use the other 30 per cent to study his surroundings. But once I pick up the canter to the first jump, I want 100-per-cent concentration.

In an outdoor competition after rain, for example, the horse may be intimidated by the footing and not want to commit himself to a solid push in order to jump the jump. Every horse conveys insecurity in a different way, but the main indicator is a loss of power in the stride. It goes dead, becomes tentative, and probably gets a little shorter. I would respond by applying more leg pressure and sitting more erect in the saddle, causing him to use his hindquarters more. To harness the new power I have just created, I would increase my contact with the mouth through the reins, by an equal and opposite amount. In other words, I use my seat, my legs, my weight, my back, to recreate the quality of gallop we need to jump the jump. I contain and regulate this power with my hands through to my horse's mouth.

Big Ben at Seoul. The green top rail blends in with the greenery below.
(Jayne Huddleston)

A horse sighting a double or triple combination of jumps might grow weak in the knees. These combinations can be built in an intimidating manner, with brightly coloured rails and lots of fill underneath them, with gates, walls, trees, or brush boxes. Colour alone can confuse a horse. Outdoors, a jump in which the highest element is a green rail may seem to the horse to blend into the backdrop of green grass. It becomes difficult for the horse to calculate the height of the jump, or perhaps his depth perception is compromised. Some say horses are colour-blind, but horses definitely react to high-gloss and flat paints and to different colours. Dull colours, and especially light brown, which horses may have trouble seeing, seem to present particular difficulty. Course designers work with all this in mind.

The insecure horse may hang back; but he may do just the opposite. He may take the bit and accelerate, dragging the rider to the jump. Whether he hangs back or attacks, I must re-establish pace and balance. If I do not, he probably cannot jump the combination, certainly not cleanly. And if I do not regain his concentration and confidence, he probably *will not* jump, or will try half-heartedly with little chance of success.

I am telling the horse, ''Remember who's the boss. And have confidence in me because I've sure told you right many more times than I've ever told you wrong. Therefore, I've earned your confidence. You know from our hours together that you've got to concentrate on me and react to what I want you to do.''

If subtle communication between us breaks down in the ring, I might touch the horse with the stick or the spur. I am issuing a little warning: ''I'm *asking* you to jump this combination. Failing that, I will *tell* you to do it. Finally, I will *demand* it.'' The horse learns to do a thing when you ask him because he wants to avoid being told; he certainly wants to avoid the demand stage. *Ask. Tell. Demand.* Each backs up the other.

The intimidation of horses — except for those rare and deplorable cases of actual abuse — works by illusion. The trainer becomes a kind of conjuror who makes the horse, weighing a thousand pounds or more, believe that his 170-pound rider actually poses a threat, one to be taken seriously. But if the trainer constantly operates in the ''demand'' phase, at best he or she is only frightening the horse into obeying. A certain chip is left on the horse's shoulder, a little nervousness or tension. An element of franticness enters the lessons, and most horses do not learn well under those conditions. Endless confrontation will ultimately diminish whatever greatness and generosity the horse has to offer. Easy to win the battle but lose the war.

To communicate with the horse, the rider uses a series of signals transmitted through the hands, legs, seat, and back, as well as upper-body angle. Messages are conveyed to the horse in varying degrees of intensity. On an arbitrary pressure scale of zero to ten degrees, a loose rein would constitute a zero-degree contact with the horse's mouth; a two-degree tension on the reins would mark a comfortable but frank contact, not unlike a handshake between two people. And a ten-degree contact would be the maximum pressure a rider could apply to the horse's mouth through the reins.

Because I like to educate my horse to listen to my whispers, that is to say, the subtleties of my messages, most of my training employs signals of five degrees or less. During training and by degrees, I lower the strength of my messages until I have taught the horse to listen to the whisper of my asking.

To repeat: I want to train sensitivity into my horse. If I am ever in a jump-off, and I go to a ten-degree leg, I will evoke a dramatic reaction, because the horse has been trained to respond to five degrees or less. But the horse should never become fearful of that ten-degree pressure — just know that it is there and respect it.

Once a horse learns this subtlety, I am in a position to use the same controls to influence his balance. Through flatwork and gymnastic exercises, I show him what balance is required to solve problems in the ring. As he learns these lessons, more and more often I leave the balance to him. In the show ring, he recognizes a circumstance, and when I add a suggestion, it has great impact.

I am also a great believer in correct technique and form, which we instil during training. If, at a competition, the horse has to compromise his form to solve a problem in the ring, I will accept that, but we will review and rebuild in our next training session. A pragmatist at heart, I believe that winning in the ring is simply a function of how careful and thorough the horse's education has been at home.

Horses, like right-handed and left-handed humans, naturally prefer to use either the right or the left side of their bodies. We train horses at Millar Brooke to be ambidextrous, so that when the horse is asked for a maximum effort (to cut in sharply, for example) on his weak side, or *lead*, there is no appreciable loss of power. Big Ben prefers the left lead, but like most grand prix horses, is almost as good on the other lead.

Some horses need help with particular jumps. When a horse knocks down a jumping rail, he may feel some discomfort, depending on how he hit it; on the other hand, he may hardly feel it at all. Planks on flat cups, for example, can be a problem. The horse quickly learns that planks come down easily, and he loses respect for them. In training, therefore, I might set a bamboo pole, called an offset, just ahead of the plank. The horse's eye is on the plank, he rubs the bamboo, and hence tries harder next time. This practice is an example of poling, which is erroneously, I believe, thought cruel, and is forbidden on showgrounds in Europe and Canada, but is allowed for all national classes in the United States. As a training technique, there is nothing wrong with poling when it is used intelligently and responsibly. One of the ironies of not allowing poling at competitions is that riders will sometimes sharpen horses in the warm-up ring by jumping them over high and wide fences, which can hurt the horse much more than a light bamboo pole would.

Some horses never require poling; they are extraordinarily careful jumpers. Some horses should not be poled at all, because it disturbs their confidence. Normally poling would only be used if a sophisticated, experienced horse had become complacent about his job. This technique, like so many other training techniques, is a method of intimidation, and the horse tends to be less and less responsive the more it is

used. During a horse's career, an offset bamboo will be effective only a certain number of times. It is, therefore, vital that he learn the lessons of carefulness while still impressed with the correction.

Developing a horse, then, is like embarking on a journey. The trainer knows where he wants to go, but remains unsure of whether the horse is capable of getting him there. The young horse may look promising as he ascends the scale in his training and competition levels, but then he encounters difficulties. The rider communicates with the horse, shows him how to solve the problem, and if the horse has the physical and mental aptitude, the problem is overcome. *En route* to the grand prix destination, problems will occasionally arise that the horse cannot solve, but a partial solution may evolve. Perhaps the rider or the horse (and horses are wonderful at this) can compensate. Some of the great grand prix horses in the world have idiosyncracies. Too many idiosyncracies, though, and the road to the grand prix ring is blocked.

A special relationship between horse and rider can be a tremendous asset in problem-solving. I can cite many instances of this, but one example, that of Brother Sam and me, will suffice. First, let me elaborate on what may seem obvious to the untrained eye, but is not: what a horse must do in a purely physical sense to jump a fence. If the jumping action of a horse's front end were to be filmed and then replayed in slow motion, you would see the horse drawing his shoulder forward and up, then drawing his forearm (from the bottom of the shoulder to the knee) forward towards his head. In flight, the forearm should be parallel with the ground. Finally his lower leg folds as tightly as possible, or as required, to the forearm.

A young or inexperienced horse may fail to use his shoulders properly and may hang the forearm down. If that happens, he must jump that much higher with his whole body in order to clear the jump. Imagine a hurdler going down the track. Hurdlers do not elevate their bodies very much. Using the most efficient method, they pull their legs

Big Ben executes a jump-off turn
(Jayne Huddleston)

Big Ben, folding his legs well at a jump.
(Jayne Huddleston)

out of the way and skim across the hurdles. In contrast, a horse must gain altitude and loft with his body; but the most efficient show-jumper, the one with good technique, also keeps his legs tight to his body as a human hurdler does. When a horse encounters jumps that truly test his power, his technique becomes crucially important for those last few inches.

In Brother Sam's case, his technique problem at the jumps was that he did not tuck in his legs tightly enough. The solution lay in the quality of his gallop, not in the jumping action itself. The horse's jump is to a great degree an extension of his canter or gallop to the jump. The more balanced his canter or gallop on the approach, the more balanced he will be at the point of take-off, and the more balanced his jump will be. Correct approach inspires correct technique. Course designers, in measuring out a distance between jumps, attempt to put a certain balance in the horse's stride that is the wrong one for the jump ahead. The trained, educated horse is able, at the point of take-off, to make the transition from one state of balance to another.

With Brother Sam, I developed an instinct that told me when he was on the verge of making a mistake in technique because of balance. Several other riders rode him but could not develop that instinct. What he and I learned together was easy for me to describe to another rider, but difficult for that rider to duplicate.

Training is work, for both me and the horse, but it is work I enjoy. Training is also part of the conditioning process. After a series of competitions, Big Ben is allowed to rest in the paddock. Like warm-blooded horses in general, he loses condition fast. A couple of weeks in the paddock, and it will take at least two weeks to get him back in shape.

The thoroughbred, on the other hand, can be out of work and on paddock rest for a long period and still be ready to show in a short time. Horsemen joke that the thoroughbred is so wired-up that even standing in his stall he keeps his shape by doing isometric exercises. All that nervous energy maintains muscle tone. The gymnastic exercises we use with show jumpers are aimed at keeping them conditioned, supple, and injury-free. If an injury occurs and the horse does not respond to conventional treatment, I sometimes bring in a chiropractor, Dr. Tom Offen, or a kinesiologist (a type of physical therapist). Dr. Offen's horse practice is a sideline; humans — me among them — are more often his patients. While veterinarians generally have their reservations about chiropractors treating horses, Dr. Offen has produced some wonderful results.

After a prolonged rest, Big Ben becomes bored by the inactivity. He stands at his stall door looking out expectantly. If I walk by and he sees that once again I'm not going to pay attention to him, he gives me a dirty look, pins his ears back, and shakes his head. He is telling me he wants to get back to work. We are a pair, he and I.

CHAPTER 11

The Life-Long Apprenticeship

With Wotan

By now it should be plain that behind many great riders there have been many great teachers. The corollary to that truth: no great rider ever *stops* being taught. Desire to learn, not necessarily natural talent, marks the truly competitive rider.

George Morris tells the story of being taken as a child by his mother to learn riding from a man named Gordon Wright at Oxridge in Connecticut. It did not take Gordon long to see that young George had no particular ability on horseback. "Are you sure he doesn't want to try some other sport?" Gordon asked Mrs. Morris, laying down the hint broadly. But no, George was back the next day, eager and determined. Gordon's method was to go slowly with his not-terribly-gifted student, which riled George but produced the best result. Those who know the sport know that George Morris went on to become one of the great riders of his day, perhaps the most analytical rider who ever lived. His book, *Hunter Seat Equitation*, first published in 1971 and revised since, remains a kind of bible to riders who want to learn classic form.

For years I wondered if George told that story to encourage young riders. Did the story downplay his own young talent to make a point? It seems not. He really did lack a natural gift. However, the desire in George Morris more than compensated for what he lacked in pure ability. Teachers warm to such desire and enthusiasm in their students. As a teacher, I love to see talent, but attitude and work habits are as important—if not more important. Talent will carry a rider a certain distance up the ladder. What happens after that depends on how badly the rider wants it.

During the Los Angeles Olympics in 1984 I watched a televised interview with a runner who had finished a marathon despite an ankle injury that would have put most people on crutches. She described the stages of a marathon: what happens in the first few kilometres, the middle leg, and finally the last part of the race. The interviewer asked her what happens at this last critical stage, and what it is that separates the winner from the rest. She simply looked at the camera and said, "It comes down to who wants it the most and who is prepared to pay the most." The way she said it gave me goose bumps, because many sports are like that. Success is the product of fierce desire. The gift, the training, and the conditioning take a rider only so far.

In the fall of 1989 I competed against thirty other riders at the Atlantic Winter Fair in Halifax, and Millar Brooke Farm took home half the prize money. We had brought Lonesome Dove, Winchester, Isis, and Pamino, leaving Big Ben and El Futuro at home to prepare for Stuttgart and the National Horse Show in New York. We did exceedingly well, then, with some of our less experienced horses. The curious thing was this: morning schooling for the horses was only allowed between 6:00 A.M. and 8:00 A.M. I was there the first morning, along with only two other riders. Where were the other twenty-seven? How easy for a rider to say the horses do not need schooling, and pass up what I considered to be a critical opportunity to train the horses in the actual competition ring.

Unwavering work habits are very important. I want to pass that discipline on to our children and to young riders. There is no sustained success without it.

Perhaps champions try so desperately to win because they fear the alternative: they are terrified of losing. I have always known this, because I feel it every day. Ron Southern, the highly successful creator of Spruce Meadows, once told me, "There isn't a deal or a business

George Morris watching the competition in Seoul with International Equestrian Federation president, Princess Anne.
(Jayne Huddleston)

venture that I enter into without feeling terrified, terrified of failure." I understood perfectly what he meant.

Fear of losing engenders a hunger for new ideas. I will always remain a student of my sport, and I know from experience that what might prove useful to me is often found in the most unlikely places. When I meet anyone, my first question is: What can I learn from this person? I am convinced that the most successful people are strong and determined, but also the most flexible. With flexibility comes the ability to change and to learn, all of which keeps me feeling young and curious. As the Toshiba commercial goes, "What separates the best from the rest is, the best keep getting better." Stand still and you get passed.

George Morris first taught me in 1973, and he taught me on several occasions thereafter, all during my tenure at Dwyer Hill. He pays me a great compliment when he calls me an ideal student who soaked up every ounce of knowledge and wisdom he had to offer. I do not teach nearly as much as I once did because of my demanding schedule, but when I do, my students are those intent on competing at my level. These are people who want to beat *me*. I know what they need to learn in order to win in the show ring, and when I recognize in riders certain moves or characteristics that will stand in their way, I am not shy about pointing them out. With students of that calibre, I keep the pressure on. If they can function with me as their teacher, the actual jumping event will be easy.

George Morris is an American grand prix rider, an internationally known coach and the author of *Hunter Seat Equitation*

Ian is very bright. We talk about using riders' aids to communicate with the horse — the hands, the voice, the whip. Many don't realize that your most important aid is your brain. Great riders also need that innate feeling for the horse. The ones who are merely good, but not great, don't have it. This innate feeling I'm talking about can't *be taught. Ian has it, Mario Deslauriers has it, Michael and John Whitaker have it. A lot of riders can think like a horse. Ian can think like the horse he's on at that moment. That's special.*

Ian's farm, Millar Brooke, is all order. You see the evidence of his discipline there. You can't name a great rider who doesn't pay that kind of attention to detail.

Ian has more strokes, more range, than other riders. His methodology is so ideal. Of anyone I have ever taught, he is closest to my ideal — in the way he exercises his horses, his work on the flat, his use of pace. He's tall, and it's important for tall riders to have form. I gave him form. He didn't have it when I began to teach him in 1973. He was a good horse-backer, but he hadn't analysed how the body should work. He was a great student, though: he absorbed everything I told him.

I'm partial to Ian because I worked with him, but his style is my ideal of a galloping, jumping style; his style and that of Mark Todd, who rides eventing [a kind of triathlon for horses that includes dressage, show jumping, and cross-country]. They represent my idea of a galloping equitation: the leg position, seat, upper body, posture, hands, and arms, all epitomize classical style. Canadian riders have a happy combination: the rugged, practical, simpler approach to riding they had before; and the polish that Ian has brought into Canada — and I hold Ian greatly responsible for the improvement in riding style in Canada. Even fifteen years ago style was pooh-poohed in Canada. Ian's is a more correct, classical style, very quiet and soft, although he can be strong. His use of aids is invisible, and that's built on classical position and form.

Big Ben will go down in history. He's a wonderful horse, but not one that crowds will look at and gasp. Horses like Jappeloup [ridden by Pierre Durand of France] and Gem Twist [ridden by Greg Best of the United States] — they create the ooohhs and aaahhs. Big Ben, he just walks around and we know *he's good. But Big Ben would have been lost without Ian.*

I distinguish in my own mind between *teaching* and *coaching*. Watching Jonathon and Amy ride in our arena and giving them guidance, I am *teaching*. I am giving them the skills that will take them up to the postgraduate level in riding. The next and higher step involves *coaching* them to use those skills in the training of horses.

To ride well, certain technical skills – position on the horse, balance, use of legs and hands, dispersal of body weight to affect the horse's balance – are a given. All good riders possess these skills. But riding becomes an art form when the rider deploys his technical riding skills to train the horse.

Imagine that a bowl of fruit is put on a table and thousands of people, all well versed in basic brush strokes and use of colour, are asked to paint the scene. One person in ten thousand will transcend his technical skills and create a work of art; the rest will simply paint a bowl of fruit. In riding, as in painting, many have the technical skill; a rare few work a kind of magic on and with horses.

Some years ago Lynn gave me *Iacocca*, the autobiography of the Chrysler Corporation president. Much of what Lee Iacocca says in that book has application in show jumping; in fact I once gave a three-day clinic in Des Moines, Iowa, based entirely on my reading of that book during the plane trip. Lee Iacocca points out that sometimes you have to make decisions without having all the facts. You have to commit yourself to a car mould, for example, before you know what the market wants.

In show jumping, and especially in a jump-off, if you slow down or add a stride (to get your bearings, to get all the "facts"), the right decision becomes the wrong decision, because by now you have lost a second and slipped to third or fourth place. On the other hand, if you gallop and turn back sharply to a jump, you come in blind. Gambling occasionally pays off. But you can also end up – as Lee Iacocca who worked for both Chrysler and Ford might say – with an Edsel.

Regardless of their natural ability, I want students to try their utmost. I get irritated by students who take shortcuts, because in show jumping there are none. I once taught a girl who was having trouble with the devil's dyke – a feature on some courses that requires horse and rider to descend into a little valley with jumps at the bottom and at one end. She had trouble with the devil's dyke during the competition because she had not bothered to do her homework by practising that fence during training. It should have been a free fence, but instead she robbed the horse of a good round for no good reason. In that situation I felt badly for the horse; with the rider I was plain irritated.

Occasionally the student's sole intention is to show the teacher how well he rides. He has an attitude problem that hinders his learning. Some riders want to learn, but have had an unstructured, undisciplined

With Amy, 1987
(Kym Ketcham)

upbringing. Teaching riders, training horses: many of the same principles apply. The first thing I establish is control, to make it clear that I am
in charge of the training session or the lesson. Some students, like some
horses, have no idea how to accept control, discipline, or criticism. It
comes as a shock. They may become belligerent, sulky, or emotional, but
I emphasize that my teaching method is not to be taken personally. I am
simply analysing them as riders physically and mentally. A disciplined
student learns not to take such analysis in a personal way.

Occasionally, a young rider will come to me for advice without
having a real stomach for the bitter pill I might prescribe. After a
frustrated rider had endured a series of disastrous competitions in 1989,
he sought my counsel. I told him that his horse had great ability, but had
lost all his confidence. Rebuild, I told him. Take the horse down a notch
to less demanding competitions and work him gradually back up to the
grand prix level. But the young rider pressed on as before, and the horse
was no closer to resolving his crisis of confidence. He had stopped
believing in himself.

With Lynn, Jonathon, and Future Vision, 1989
(James Leslie Parker)

I find teaching both rewarding and exhausting. My students are advanced, and I find it a rigorous task to dissect simultaneously the student's style of riding, his or her emotional and mental attitude towards riding, as well as the horse's physical gifts, his strengths and limitations, and his state of mind. I may select a training sequence to correct any problem. I then teach the student how to apply the correction, when to stay with repetition, and when to escalate the pressure behind the correction. To avoid discouragement, I also tell him how long he should stay with the repetition before he can expect a result. At some point, it may be time to move on to another method.

We have had quite a number of resident riders at Millar Brooke over the years, some from as far away as Korea and Mexico. In their early to mid-twenties, they essentially receive a university education in horsemanship. They get room, board, and expenses, and about $15,000 a year for working what I jokingly call half-days — 7:00 A.M. to 7:00 P.M. Sometimes their parents remark on the change that has taken place in their sons and daughters. The students learn not just riding skills but a set of standards that govern how they think and behave. I once had a young female rider who only called home after she had done well at a show — never after she had done badly. I told her, "You've got to understand. Your parents are your backers. It's a familial, but also a business relationship. Call when things go badly as well as when they go well."

I want students to understand the dedication and inherent responsibilities required to do well in the sport. I do expect a lot from them, certainly from those with ambition, and over time, they begin to see the great canyon between mediocrity and excellence. Not many are willing to make the leap.

181

I tell students the ingredients I think go into the making of a good rider, even though some might find it discouraging to hear. My measure of a good rider, and therefore of a good horseman, is strict and all-inclusive: How well does he ride? Train horses? Care for and manage a horse, physically and mentally? What kind of strategist is the rider? Which classes does he or she select to develop the horse properly and to make him shine when the rider wants him to shine? How does the rider deal with owners and investors? What about business skills? I look at how the equipment, the trucks, and the trailers, are maintained. Every aspect counts. There is nothing on my own farm that I cannot do, from driving heavy machinery and tractor trailers to grooming a horse and running the business. Not many other sports demand that their athletes possess that range.

Good riders are consummate horsemen or horsewomen. They have to know their horses, who cannot, after all, talk. When a blacksmith or a veterinarian needs to know something about a horse, the rider and the groom talk on the horse's behalf.

Self-control, I tell students, is another must. If a rider allows his emotions to creep in, especially during a competition, his horse will definitely be affected. If the rider is nervous or angry or afraid, the horse will know; he will sense the emotion. Self-control is just as important in the training of a horse. A trainer's character flaws will surely be reflected in the horse. Lose your temper with a horse, for example, and you may have wiped out months of work. I stopped losing my temper with horses when I was nineteen or twenty years old.

The good rider is also a finely tuned athlete. His reflexes have to be as fast as greased lightning. If not, he will often find himself on the ground. When a horse begins to stumble or slip, the slightest shift in the rider's weight and balance will determine whether he is launched out of the tack or stays put.

Line up a dozen grand prix riders, ask them to run the mile and you will not find many speed demons. But ask the same twelve to ride a series of different horses for eight or ten hours and they will have no difficulty. (Anyone who has ridden knows how taxing this can be.) Afterwards they can dance all night and ride for eight more hours the next day. Strength is not so important. Certain parts of my legs, back, and arms are strong, but if brute strength is required to ride a horse, then my training has not accomplished what it should have. Technique and finesse are more important. When I leave the ring, I am normally not drawing a deep breath.

Also critical is the rider's ability to read the ground, to calculate distance. To have a "rider's eye", as it is called, is to have the ability to look at the jump down the ring, five to seven strides away, and know what adjustments have to be made in the stride to arrive at the right place at the right time. Younger, green riders do not see the distance at all. They will gallop right up to the fence, jump it, and gallop away. If you ask them afterwards, "Did you see a distance?" they say, "No. My horse found the distance," or "It just worked out." Riders can take years and years to develop the skill, and some never do.

After Gail Greenough became the first Canadian and the first woman ever to win the world championship in show jumping in 1986, I wrote an article about that feat. The piece started with some thoughts on how riders learn: from horses, from teachers, and from the examples of others. Europeans tend to learn almost totally from horses and other riders. Americans learn most from being taught. In Canada, we tend to benefit from all three resources. But young riders may take time to learn this.

Jim Elder
(Jayne Huddleston)

I think back to the Spruce Meadows Masters Tournament in the fall of 1989. It was clear to me in several classes that the horses of a young Canadian team rider were undercaulked. The sloppy footing meant that the horses needed the help of bigger cleats. Why had the rider not sought my advice or someone else's on this matter of caulking? Perhaps the rider had a fear of being rebuffed; I did not feel it was my place to offer advice when none was sought. I am sure the rider will learn from that experience.

If I were to tell one student in a riding clinic that his leg is too far forward, I would want the six or seven others there to ask themselves if the point applied to them too. I try to teach young riders to be good students of the sport and never to pass up an opportunity to learn.

Carefully watching other riders can in itself be a learning experience. I first became involved in show jumping in the Ottawa area; then I graduated to shows around Montreal. After that I began to compete around Toronto, then on to the United States, and eventually the international circuits. At each level, I had the opportunity to watch, and ride against, certain riders who, in effect, became my teachers. In Montreal there were Valaire Francours, Jacques Ferland, and Max Bidner. There was an American named Sonny Brooks, who introduced a whole new range of techniques. No one could seem to beat him. We watched and learned from him, and soon we were beating him sometimes. In the Toronto area, Jimmy Elder, Jimmy Day, and Tom Gayford were great influences. In the United States, Rodney Jenkins, Bernie Traurig, George Morris, Michael Matz, Dennis Murphy. And then as we started to see Europe: Hans Günter Winkler, Hartwig Steenken, Paul and Alwin Schockemöhle, David Broome, Harvey Smith, Eddie Macken, John and Michael Whitaker, Nick Skelton, Nelson Pessoa, Emile Hendrix, Hugo Simon, and many more.

Nick Skelton, British grand prix rider, former European Junior Champion

To be a great rider you've got to be quiet, you must have a good eye for speed and distance. Whatever stride your horse is taking, you've got to see exactly when you're going to take off, you need good hands, you have to be brave (especially in jump-offs), and you have to have the will to win.

Ian is one of the top five jockeys in the world. It's not fair to pick out one from the other. Who knows who is the best? But he has all those qualities I've just listed. To be a great jockey you have to win on every horse that comes by, not just the one big horse. John Whitaker, for instance, has won on Ryan's Son, on Gammon, on Milton. Ian is the same. The class is never won until he's finished.

Big Ben, for such a big horse, is very short, which helps him a great deal. He's tall, but not long. He's always compact, and he's got just a huge jump. He's careful, and fast.

Another thing that Ian can do is ride difficult horses, ones that don't suit other people. That's also part of being a great jockey: that feeling for a horse. If the horse is quick, you have to sit quiet; if he's a little bit slow you have to ride him up a bit, squeeze him with a bit more leg; if he's a bit slow in front you keep him off; if he's quick in front you ride him close. You have to get a feel. It's a gift you're born with, and Ian has it.

In our sport, at this level, necessity truly is the mother of invention. You watch how other riders solve particular problems, because down the line you may have that very same problem in an otherwise wonderful horse. Then you already have the solution, and you have it, free and simple, by watching great riders ride.

My own style of teaching is based on this credo: *Let design follow function*. If I were an architect designing a multi-level building for older people, I would include elevators. If I installed stairs because they looked nice, then design would not follow function. I look at riding position, stirrup length, upper-body angulation, and rein length in the same way. I must be able to answer the question, "Why is my way the best way?" with this answer: "Because it's the most functional and the most effective." Often, the exercise of teaching forces the rider into a close examination of his own ideas and habits. Sometimes I will correct a

At a press conference at
Spruce Meadows, with
Laura Balisky (left) and
Linda Southern
(Andy Rose)

habit in a student, and I will say to Lynn, "Where did that come from?"
And she will answer, "Well, have you looked in the mirror lately?"

My own riding in the show ring is not something I consciously think
about, no more than a professional hockey player would think about his
skating during a game. I aim to be a quiet, soft, and passive rider. I wear
glasses but they never slip off: my ankles, knees, and hips act like shock-
absorbers. I believe in efficiency of riding. With that comes simplifica-
tion. The less you do on a horse, the simpler it is, the more you leave to
him. So often I will see a rider take a rail down, and I will think, "If only
he had sat still."

Show jumping is one of the few sports in which men and women
compete on an equal basis. Some of the women riders I have admired are
the Belgian rider Evelyn Blaton, Americans Leslie Burr Lenehan, Katie
Monahan Prudent, Debbie Schaffner, and Susan Hutchison, Britain's Liz
Edgar, and Canada's Laura Balisky, Gail Greenough, and Lisa Carlsen.

In general, male and female riders adopt profoundly different
approaches. Young and even mature female riders tend to become more
emotionally entwined with the horse than males do. Gentle persuasion,
they think, works best. Males, on the other hand, tend to try force
first: the bigger-hammer theory. In fact, the best riders are capable of
deploying both tactics. My experience with young people has taught me
that, in general, I have to teach young women to become stricter, more
consistent disciplinarians. Young men, on the other hand, need to learn
more patience and sympathy for the horse. They are not on motorcycles,
I tell them, but on living, breathing animals with moods and emotions.

Women, in North America at least, are at no disadvantage in show
jumping. If you train sensitivity into your horse, no great strength is
required. However, an accomplished male rider who has learned tact can
probably ride a wider range of horses because of his size and strength.

Laura Balisky, Canadian grand prix rider

I've spent a lot of time as a student of Ian's, starting in 1984 at Millar Brooke. I've been his friend ever since, and I remain one of his pupils. As a teacher, he's brilliant in the way that he thinks so deeply about everything — from the minds of the horses he'll ride the next day to the courses he'll set out for them. He would always tell me that there are many little 1 per cents in the sport — the blacksmith is 1 per cent, the barn staff is 1 per cent, your training of the horse is 1 per cent. Ian is himself full of little 1 per cents. In Nations' Cup competitions, or whenever I've sought his advice, he's been generous and caring.

What makes him special in the ring is that he's so methodical. He's such a trained person. At the World Cup Final, for example, where he has enjoyed just phenomenal success, he's always mentally prepared, working on his checklist. He's trained himself to be perceptive to every detail.

In the horse business a lot of riders ride off their talent. Not Ian. There's no doubt about his talent; it's just that he doesn't rely totally on it. He's one of the most goal-oriented people I've ever met. When he enters the ring he doesn't want to settle for second-best. Many riders lack that confidence.

He has an amazing gift for getting on horses and getting along with them. He rides so many different types of horses. Ian really is at the pinnacle in our sport, and it's hard for most people to understand what that means. If he was a hockey player, he would have Gretzky status.

Many girls want to make a friend of the horse first, thinking that this will encourage the horse to do their bidding. I tell them — and sometimes they are alarmed to hear this — that a horse is not a teddy bear or a house pet but a thousand pounds of strong, wilful animal. Just because you love him does not mean that he loves you. I teach these students not only how to ride, but also how to train horses. I explain that the first task is take control of the horse. Once that is accomplished, you teach him what he needs to know. When he is controlled, obedient, and knowledgeable, *then* make him a friend. Out of that friendship comes the greatness.

Big Ben and I, for example, do not cozy up to one another any more than a police dog would sit in the lap of his handler while both watch TV in the evening. Ben is a trained professional in his own right, a highly skilled, elite athlete. He has an ego, a temper, and determination. Ours is a disciplined, structured, working relationship. We are two players who show mutual respect for each other, playing on the same team. But I am also the coach and the quarterback who ultimately calls the plays.

Certain people should never be taught by a perfectionist like me: my spouse, for example. When Lynn and I were quite young, I set out to make her a great rider, a mistake that onlookers, at least, found amusing.

In a way Lynn is my personal *chef d'équipe*. From the ground she has a unique vantage point on horse and rider, and her commentary during training, during the warm-up before the competition, and afterwards is critically important. It is her job to point out my mistakes, and over the years I can think of no occasion when she has not conveyed the right message and at the right time. I always get the truth. When I tried to teach Lynn to ride, I lacked that diplomacy and tact and sense of timing. I wanted only that she ride well. Lynn, on the other hand, wanted companionship, not preparation for the Olympic Games. I botched the job, with the result that Lynn does not ride now. Occasionally I try to coax her onto a horse, but she has no interest. I feel badly about that, very badly.

(Tish Quirk)

Perhaps I learned from that episode. Amy, for example, has been taught at horse shows by Barb Mitchell of Toronto and in Florida by Trudy Glefke. Instruction should come from an objective observer. Often parents cannot do the job; their guidance is too open to emotional interpretation on both sides. More recently, though, I started teaching the children at home. Clearly they have matured and learned lesson etiquette.

Both Amy and Jonathon are fine riders. Jonathon (my nickname for him is "Chief", because when he was born he was foremost in our lives) tends to pick riding up and then put it down. In the summer of 1989, however, he entered a horse in a division called "hopeful jumpers" and did very well. Amy became serious about riding at the age of nine and has been hard at it ever since.

I do not encourage our children to consider the sport as a career, but neither do I discourage them. Life with horses is tremendously rich and rewarding – if, but only if, a life with horses is what you want and love.

I could not do what I do without Lynn. An unusual woman in every regard, she balances a home and a road life, cares for two children, and helps me with owners and staff. She is made of steel. Amy and Jonathon would each need that kind of partner, with a similar kind of love for the sport. A labour of love, a lifestyle, a hobby, work: show jumping is all that and more. A rider's life is not a normal life. Only a handful of people do very, very well financially in the sport; many more have a substantial cash flow, but not much to show for their trouble by the end of the year.

Having fun at Spruce Meadows with well-known British journalist Peter Churchill
(Tish Quirk)

And yet, a great many people are drawn to show jumping. There are intangible rewards to a life with horses. Perhaps this is one: it keeps me young. I meet people my own age outside the horse world and they seem so much older to me than I seem to myself. Why is that? I can feel boyish in their company. David Broome, the forty-nine-year-old British rider, told me in Stuttgart that he finds himself addressing people younger than himself as "Sir". Sometimes it seems that many of my contemporaries outside the horse world have lost their senses of humour. They, on the other hand, are probably wondering, "When is Ian Millar going to get a real job and grow up?"

Winning in grand prix show jumping is for the young at heart, and I will know it when I no longer feel young. But I do not see that happening for a long while.

CHAPTER 12

The Royal (and Shows Within Shows)

The contrast between the two rings is sharp. Look first in the main arena of the Coliseum. The Royal Winter Fair in Toronto is among the most prestigious indoor show-jumping events in North America. Its preferred red box-seats are filled this November evening with men in tuxedos, ladies in daring evening gowns, and young debutantes. Wealthy patrons of show jumping are here to see, and to be seen.

(Jayne Huddleston)

189

Now look in the small hitching ring that feeds into the arena. I am here taking a horse over practice jumps, but I am never alone in this busy ring. Running its length and set off by a single-rail fence is a thoroughfare for pedestrians – farmers in baseball caps, young girls in jodhpurs, and grooms looking tired and rumpled, with blankets and show coolers over their shoulders. Horses and riders of all sizes and kinds occupy the hitching ring during the eleven-day fair. On some of these days, being in the hitching ring is like being backstage at an epic play, or on the set of *The Wizard of Oz*. I note, for example, a diminutive Tin Man and Cowardly Lion, an Appaloosa ridden by an "Indian" boy-warrior in full ceremonial headdress, tiny nuns and pirates, and miniature horses no higher than my kneecap, all gathered where sliding doors open out to an adjacent walking ring in the mezzanine. The walking ring, with low stands on either side, blends into the fair's marketplace, where everything from tack and horse equipment to cars and lounge chairs are on display. This is the stage where little players on little horses perform.

At the Royal there are shows, and shows within shows.

Like its predecessors, the 1989 Royal Winter Fair is an agricultural fair, a trade show, and a horse show all at the same time. From shaggy giant Clydesdales to sleek grand prix horses, from sculpted butter to equine sculpture, from Mennonite sausages to displays on composting, the Royal is that uniquely Canadian place where city meets country.

There are only four Nations' Cup events in North America, two in Canada, and two in the United States. Spruce Meadows has one, the Royal has another. As a team and as individuals, Canadian riders want to do well here, and for all kinds of reasons. The Royal is, for us, centre stage. Everything we do is visible. The hometown crowd wants us to do well, media coverage is extensive. Corporate sponsors and prospective sponsors for both the team and individual riders are watching. More owners attend the Royal than any other Canadian show. All eyes are on us.

At times great things have happened at the Royal to both the Canadian equestrian team and to me as an individual rider. But at other times it has seemed that Murphy's Law prevails.

One year, there was a two-horse class: a groom leads the second horse in, and after the rider has jumped the course one way, he leaps onto the back of the second horse and rides the course the opposite way. At home I had practised the exchange – which requires that both horses stand perfectly still beside each other as I jump from the back of one to the back of the other – and it had always gone well.

I sped around first on a horse called Another Brother, and went clear. But as I approached my second horse, a "mare-ish", moody

Walking the course with Lt.-Gov. Lincoln Alexander and then President of the Royal Winter Fair, Moffat Dunlap

gelding named Bandit, I noticed that he had cocked his head, and his ears were pinned halfway back. This was a look I had not seen before. As we got close, Bandit aimed a kick at Another Brother, scoring a hit on the chest. With my first horse unhurt but no longer willing to go near the second horse, I was forced to dismount and run after Bandit. A possible first prize thus became a disappointing fifth.

At another Royal I was riding an extremely sharp and agile speed horse called Lucas. One course featured a tight inside turn, and I was cantering *past* a wall when suddenly Lucas left the ground and jumped the wall — sideways. When I watched it later on a video I could scarcely believe my eyes. It seemed as if he had pushed off with his left front and left hind legs. With me eliminated and the audience convulsed with laughter, Mr. Murphy and his famous law had chalked up another victory.

This Sixty-first Royal is no exception. Early in the competition, I rode in the high-score class in which the rider chooses his or her own course. The fences, which are assigned different values, can be jumped up to two times each, and in any order within the fifty-second time limit. The object is to jump as many high-point fences as possible, but the rider has to be in the air to gain the last fence when the buzzer sounds at the fifty-second mark. A fuss erupted when the judges ruled that my horse was *not* in the air. I maintained we were in the air, and half the people I talked to afterwards agreed. However, the other half were not convinced. The crowd did not like the call one bit. Several years ago Mario Deslauriers and I were paired in a costume-class relay, and again there was a judgement call that had the crowd booing vigorously — and for the Royal, quite uncharacteristically.

The Royal, then, can spell tough luck — even for the home team.

Canada last won a Nations' Cup at the Royal in 1979; to win on the tenth anniversary of our last victory would have been fitting. On the first Saturday of the fair we came tantalizingly close to doing just that. The team of Mario Deslauriers on Box Car Willie, Lisa Carlsen on Kahlua, Hugh Graham on Sirocco, and me on Big Ben certainly had the experience. But after two rounds, including a double-clear by Big Ben, we were tied with the British at eight faults, and that rare thing occurred, a Nations' Cup jump-off — which we lost.

Had the Canadian team knocked down one less rail, or the British team one more rail, during the first two rounds, we would have won, with no need for a jump-off. The crowd had cheered our every move. Everybody had cheered but Mr. Murphy.

The week had also begun badly for Millar Brooke Farm. After shows in Stuttgart and New York, I returned to the farm on a Monday, hoping for some rest before going to the Royal on Wednesday. There would be no rest: chaos awaited me. The phone rang unceasingly, a groom resigned, several owners dropped in for long talks, and details of the next two European shows (Bordeaux and Brussels) seemed to change every thirty minutes. It was 3:00 P.M. Monday before I even started to school the horses, six hours behind schedule.

I came to the Royal, then, hoping to find yet-untapped springs of energy in my body. But morning schooling on the first day began disastrously: someone let in an army of junior riders, and instead of the allotted sixteen riders in the practice ring there were forty-five.

Early in the fair, Amy rode in what's called the pony working hunter division, the championship to be decided by the results in four classes. Her first class began the way my week had begun: no points. She was despondent as a result. But I took her aside and told her that the judging in the hunter class was a subjective matter, one person's opinion; that her job in the remaining classes was to outride every other rider, to ride so well she could not be denied the prize. In the next class the judge was absolutely won over by her near-perfect performance. She took my breath away too. She won that class, and the one after that, and finally the championship. All of us in the Millar Brooke camp were elated by Amy's biggest victory so far.

After its classes, Amy's pony was moved out of the Royal, thus freeing up a stall. I grabbed it. This would be my retreat for the rest of the fair. We threw up heavy blue canvas, called tack-room curtains, around the stall — without any Millar Brooke lettering or indeed any hint that this was home to Ian Millar — put in a cot and a small table, and drove a nail into a board at eye level so I could hang up my red coat and riding hat. It was not a quiet retreat — the clucking and honking of the poultry next door, general stable noise, and loudspeakers continued unabated — but at least I had a place to go when solitude became important.

The Canadian equestrian team stable, with its distinctive red-and-white pin stripes, is as much a part of the fair as the prize ducks and roosters who were our neighbours. At any time of the day, dozens of fair-goers gathered around Big Ben's stall, some of them quite oblivious to the danger that exists when horses are confined in a noisy, poorly ventilated stable for an extended period and subjected to sometimes unwanted attention. Early in the fair, Big Ben was standing cross-tied (secured by lines on either side of the halter) in the grooming stall, when a father placed his two pre-school sons directly in front of the horse so Dad could take a photo. The man completely ignored Sandi's warning and proceeded with the photo while Big Ben pawed the ground. Soon after that, we put up barriers to give Big Ben and the other Canadian-team horses some breathing room.

The grooms' daily work around the horses, which can be dangerous at the best of times, gets more so at shows such as the Royal. Horses loathe surprises — someone shaking an umbrella, a child with a balloon, sudden noises — and a groom working around a horse's leg is quite vulnerable when a horse spooks.

Some grooms put up menacing signs in front of stalls to discourage patting. "This horse enjoys little childrens' fingers more than oats," read one. Either the horse was indeed feisty, or the groom had become so. One year at the Royal, a groom, weary of giving directions to Big Ben's stall, laid down masking-tape arrows on the concrete leading to his stall.

Show jumping has undergone a dramatic transition. Where once there were followers of the sport, now there are fans seeking out individual horses and riders. They want photos of me and/or Big Ben, autographs, a bit of conversation. Some want souvenirs. Two days into the event, Sandi was lamenting that a souvenir-hunter had made off with Big Ben's halter. (A harness-maker who supplies the Canadian equestrian team kindly replaced it.) The Bank of Montreal hit upon an idea to raise funds for the Canadian equestrian team at the Royal. They offered a chance for fans to have a Polaroid photo taken with Ian Millar and Big Ben — actually life-sized cutouts — and charged a $2 minimum. The gimmick drew a steady line of takers and raised $1,200.

I do love to talk to fans at the Royal, and especially young ones with their own horse stories to tell, but all that activity can get in the way of

Big Ben peers out of the temporary stall that he lives in at a horse show.
(John Graydon)

riding. Merely passing instructions to Sandi and getting her input can be difficult to achieve without interruption if we attempt it near the Canadian team stall. The demands on a rider's time at the Royal — Canadian Equestrian Federation meetings, banquets, meetings with sponsors, agents, and journalists — can make it difficult to find adequate time to ride.

Into the third and fourth day of the Sixty-first Royal, grooms and riders began to get what some call "the Royal grippe": a hacking cough and sore throat, commonly blamed on the pungent air in the Coliseum. In the interests of heating, the windows are for the most part closed off, and barn air takes over.

There are evening classes at the Royal, and when the show runs behind schedule, as it often does, there is less time for sleep. Run-down bodies fall prey to the grippe. One night, after a jump-off, it was 2:00 A.M. before I got to bed. Supper was a room-service hamburger and a Perrier. I woke up three and a half hours later. Although I pride myself on never getting sick, the night before the grand prix event at this Royal, I was up all night with the flu. But the show must go on, and it does.

Boys and girls dressed as pirates and nuns. Men and women sporting leather and furs. Everybody at the Royal, it seems, is in costume. Even riders. One of the celebrated features at the Royal horse show, as at many others, is the costume class in which riders compete, not in their formal blue or red coats, but dressed up as clowns or animals. There is no middle opinion on the costume class: either you love it or you hate it.

Those opposed argue that a well-known rider dressed up as Batman suffers a loss of dignity. If there must be a costume class, they insist, run it as a matinée and not on a Saturday night when pure show jumping should be offered.

Those in favour believe that riders should be allowed to let loose and have fun in the ring. But do riders actually enjoy it? Not many do, and I'm among them. People want to see us ride; if they want comedy they should go see comedians. Imagine going to watch a highly regarded comedian and having him suddenly announce, "Tonight I'm not going to tell jokes. Tonight I'm going to ride a horse." At the Sixty-first Royal the costume class is mandatory for riders. The entire Canadian equestrian team came out dressed as "super-dogs" (the canine equivalent of grand prix horses, dog shows being a feature of many horse shows). With me as "trainer" we did our dogged best, but neither the skit nor our costumes took a prize.

There are some observers, such as Ron Southern of Spruce Meadows, who believe that those other costumes — tuxedos and fancy gowns — imply that show jumping remains the preserve of the privileged and thus do a great disservice to the sport. On this issue I *do* take the middle position. I like what works. The horse show in Cincinatti is held in a football stadium and features a charity dinner at $1,000 a plate. With valet parking and other appropriate touches, the dinner raises about $700,000 for a local hospital. That kind of thing would never work at Spruce Meadows; it would seem out of character in Alberta. But in Toronto the black ties and long dresses are as much a tradition at the Royal as ribbons and judges.

In 1975 I rode at the Royal in a fibreglass, hinged cast. I had broken my arm at the Pan-American Games in Mexico beforehand. While I was practising the day before the Games, my second horse, the aforementioned Bandit, stopped suddenly in front of a jump, and I slid out of the saddle and over his shoulder. The rail came down and broke both bones in my arm. Clearly the broken arm affected my performance at the Royal that year. If I was hurt today and forced to compete in a cast, would I do so? Well, yes. Call it Millar's Definition of Maturity: back then I did not know better, and therefore competed. Now I do know better and I would *still* go ahead and compete.

At that Royal my cast was a visible reminder to everyone watching that the sport can be a dangerous one. I once had a horse called Foxfire. A "kidney stud" — a gelded horse, but with one testicle left in his body — he was a wonderful jumper, but a very aggressive horse; even tacking him up was hazardous. Of all the horses I have worked with, only Foxfire would chase you out of his paddock. I rode him, but I always told Lynn and the grooms that if he ever bucked me off, they were to get him away from me as best they could.

Courage *does* separate good from great riders. There is no rider at the elite level who has not endured his or her share of terrible falls and broken bones. The one who wins knows the fine line between what is possible and what is not, and has ridden on that line without fear. Winners take risks without dwelling on possible consequences. In baseball, the big home-run hitters tend to strike out the most. Our sport is the same: good riders have had their share of disaster.

I seem not to be able to remember dreams, but falls from horses stay in my mind and have the quality of dreams. I am like a race-car driver who can recall the few seconds leading up to a crash and talk about it in precise detail for thirty minutes. Similarly, a twenty-five-second jump-off, or any dramatic moment in the ring, can live on in my mind like an unforgettable film.

At a competition in Sutton, Ontario, in 1981 the then-young Warrior, with me in the saddle, fell in spectacular fashion. As we were rolling on the ground, one of his caulks came around and caught me on the chin, opening up a bloody gash. I was led off the field, and a good friend from the Dwyer Hill days, Barry Collard, took me into the show trailer and patched me up. He put tape down each side of the wound, cotton batten right on the wound, and finally ran tape across to close it up. Then he said, "Go finish the class." I went back, and won the class, with blood running down my face and onto my shirt and coat.

Then Barry took me to the local doctor. It was a Sunday night, about 6:00 P.M., and I asked the physician if I needed plastic surgery. "Hell, no," he said, assuring me that every Friday and Saturday night the locals drank too much, fought, and cut each other up, and that he did lots of this kind of work. Every time I see Barry to this day, he examines the scar on my chin and he says, "We did all right."

Sometimes the injuries are far more severe. George Morris, for example, continues to ride, despite separate falls that have broken his leg and vertebrae in his neck.

Riding with a fibreglass cast, hinged at the elbow
(Maria Prezyna)

At Spruce Meadows in 1978 the footing was bad and my horse, Brother Sam, stopped and slid sideways at the same time, throwing me backwards into the standard. Later, in the hospital, a doctor with an odd bedside manner told me bluntly, "You have a broken back." (This was a gross exaggeration as it turned out. Actually, it was a broken transverse process, one of the finger-like bones that emanate from the spinal column.) "Can you inject it with something to dull the pain?" I asked him. He said he would give me painkillers, but nothing that would affect balance or depth perception. This occurred on the first day of the horse show, and the rules forbade substitute riders. Not wanting to let anyone down, I rode, but I was in agony most of the week. I recovered, and two years later X-rays showed no evidence that the bone had been broken, so nicely had it healed.

More recently, in Florida during the winter of 1988, one of my horses flipped over, then rolled the length of me as I lay on the ground. Precisely the same thing had happened on another occasion. Years ago, we had a horse called O Henry who could kick his hind end to the moon. He landed after a jump at too steep an angle – more like eighty degrees than forty-five degrees – and when he flipped those hind feet (to the moon, of course), his front feet could not get out of the way quickly enough. He pitched forward until he was on his forehead, perpendicular to the ground, and I was catapulted from the saddle. I remember skidding along face-first and thinking, "I wonder where O Henry is." I found out. Tumbling on the ground, he came up the length of me, like a rolling pin, straight into the small of my back, where he finally stopped.

A fall that a stunt man
would have been proud of
(Harry Gerke)

Everybody ran out onto the field, and someone jumped on O Henry's head to stop him from getting up suddenly and exacerbating my injury. Then it was decided that O Henry should be allowed to get up, which he did, very daintily, while I covered my head with my hands. The pain was unbelievable; I worried that both ankles were broken. Tom Gayford said, "Quickly, quickly, we've got to cut those boots off." Now, those boots cost about five hundred dollars, and I was not about to have them cut. Slowly I got up. I knew that, if I took off the boots, the swelling would never allow me to get them back on. And so, whether in the saddle or asleep in bed, I kept my boots and britches on for the two remaining days of the horse show.

I did things in my youth that only a brash and sometimes reckless seventeen-year-old would attempt. I had a horse who would not be careful about jumps. He thought that knocking them down was a game. So I said to myself, "I'm going to fix you." I got two posts and tied a rail to them in such a way that it could not fall down, a big heavy rail. Toward this thing we raced, the horse and I, and when he hit it, he flipped over, pitching me onto the frozen ground before landing on top of me. I rolled over, and found there was no feeling in my legs. Luckily no one was home; my mother would not have been pleased. I remember being very concerned—I do not remember panic. After what seemed like a long time, a tingling sensation started in my legs, and the feeling came back. I got back on the horse and retied the rail so that one end would fall down and went at it again.

Even working around horses leaves one vulnerable to injury. At Mrs. Gardiner's stable in Edmonton I had to tack up a horse standing at the back of the stall, a difficult young horse. I went in, closed the lock on the bottom part of the Dutch door, approached the horse with saddle and saddle pad in hand, and walked straight up to where the saddle would go. One should always approach a horse at the shoulder; I should have done

Attending the school of hard knocks
(Ian Christie)

a detour and traced the wall. I never saw it coming, but the mare gave me a mighty kick. I woke up lying on the ground on top of the bottom half of the Dutch door. My trajectory had taken the door right off the hinges, and my first sight upon regaining consciousness was the mare standing in the stall looking at me.

Although I was in extreme pain, I did not want anyone to know about the accident. I realized immediately that it was my own fault. Somehow I got through that week without telling anyone.

Sometimes, the courage needed to be a good rider is simply the courage required to risk making a fool of yourself while thousands of people look on. I remember competing in Harrisburg, Pennsylvania, when I was twenty-four. In a particular class called "the gambler's choice", the jumps were each assigned points according to their difficulty, and the rider could jump them in any order, and no more than twice within the time allowed. The rider with the most points, obviously, won. But the rule was that if you knocked down a rail, it stayed down. You had sixty seconds to complete the round. I went raging around the course on War Machine, and within thirty seconds I had knocked down every rail. There was nothing left to jump. There I was, pulled up in the middle of the ring, thoroughly embarrassed. I tipped my hat and left.

I look back on these and other occasions early in my career and I think how amazingly resilient I was. I could enter one class and the result would be calamitous, but by the very next class I was absolutely convinced I would win. In my sport, 90 per cent of the time that riders enter the show ring, they lose. The young Canadian rider Harold Chopping once said, and this was very astute on his part, that riders are "tragically optimistic".

Riders, for example, would prefer not to contemplate the possibility of their horses dying. But horses do die prematurely, and sometimes, though it is fortunately rare, during competition. Every year arena staff at the Royal practise for just such an eventuality. Some years ago a horse died here in the ring. A tall shroud was erected around the horse so that he could be taken away with dignity.

I have seen a number of horses die, and each death has been a traumatic event. Once at Millar Brooke a mare called Saskia was discovered at 1:30 in the morning suffering dreadfully from colic, the intestinal blockage that is the single biggest killer of horses. We did everything we could, but four hours later she was dead.

In competition I have only lost one horse, and that was at Sutton in 1985. We had come to the last jump, a triple combination. The horse, a bay thoroughbred named Largo, took a strange step and came off the ground to the first jump — again in an odd manner — then he hit the next jump and stopped before the last one. I could feel he was on three legs, and as I looked over I saw one leg swinging loosely, almost like a broken picket fence in a strong wind. I jumped off immediately, while other riders and trainers brought over jump standards (the wooden supports for fences); using blankets and coolers, we made a shroud. Because the horse was in terrible pain, the vets gave him medication and then euthanized him on the spot. We lifted his body into the bucket of a tractor, covered him with blankets, and took him out of the ring. Later the body was taken to the Ontario Veterinary College at the University of Guelph for an autopsy, which revealed that the bone had shattered beyond any hope of mending. The reason why remains a mystery. Was it a weakness in the leg? A freak landing?

I felt a terrible sadness. The suddenness was devastating. One minute I was on a dynamic, high-performance horse, and the next he had a broken leg. My rational mind *knew* that the horse had to be euthanized, but my heart asked, "Can't *something* be done?" I also felt a tremendous personal responsibility, because left to his own devices that horse would have been out in a field eating grass.

I compete at the Royal and at many other shows, but I also conduct horse business there. I am always on the lookout for a horse to buy, or maybe a chance to sell one of my own. At this Royal, for example, Pamino, a wonderful mare who had done particularly well in both Toronto and New York, attracted some attention. As her rider and trainer, I am duty-bound to pass on any offers of purchase to her American owners. Selling an admirable horse is not easy; it was even tougher when I was young. If I fall in love with a horse, that is *my* problem. However, I invariably fall in love with the good ones.

Buying a good horse is trickier still. In a horse deal, you are always vulnerable. There are things you cannot know about a horse until you have lived with him for a month or more. You have to trust the seller's answers to your questions, and if the seller is not trustworthy, you are in trouble. (On the other hand, as I have said, I would never let my lack of confidence in a seller stand in the way of buying a good horse.)

I once bought a horse in France for a young and somewhat inexperienced rider in Canada, all of which I explained to the seller, who assured me that the horse was suitable. When I rode him, the horse seemed, to use the horseman's term, soft in my hands: a cooperative, controlled horse. But like car-dealers who put sawdust in bad transmissions to mask problems, an unethical horse-dealer has tricks. He can tranquilize the horse before the buyer comes, work him for hours beforehand, or take the horse's water away for a day — all deplorable tactics. In any case, the seller lied to me.

The minute I rode the horse at home, I could feel he was too strong for the intended rider. I had spent a great deal of money on a horse meant to do a particular job, and clearly he was not right for the job. I am not a vengeful person, but I made sure I got even with that seller; I made no secret of the fact that I had been lied to.

Horse-dealing is a cleaner business than it used to be, but there are still many ways to lose your shirt. Horses do not come with neat price stickers on them; as in most purchases, the buyer must beware. Often the deal is struck by two horse trainers acting as agents, one for the buyer, one for the seller. This is especially true of costly grand prix horses. The seller's agent is supposed to answer truthfully all questions about the horse's strengths and weaknesses. He can make the horse bigger than life, and pull off the sale, but soon enough his reputation is sullied. Both the buyer and his own agent certainly want the truth about the horse, especially if the agent faces the task of training the horse. If the horse is not exactly as advertised, the trainer can look forward to endless work and frustration. The long-term incentive on both sides, then, is to tell the truth. Certain checks and balances are in place to ensure honest horse-trading.

Problems occur when both agents conspire to take a profit on the deal. Each agent uses the other as a cover, but they share in the kickback. When the deal is worth $750,000, the temptation to take a cut may seem irresistible to some horsemen. A "double commission", as it's sometimes called (taking a commission from both the buyer and the seller) constitutes fraud. But in general, most horse deals are fine.

For me, the rule in horse dealing is always the same: as much as possible I have to trust the seller. About 70 per cent of the horses I have bought in Europe, including Big Ben of course, have come through Emile Hendrix. I have faith in him.

When I buy a horse — and I have bought hundreds — I gather first impressions. I look for quality in appearance, not necessarily beauty. I check his conformation, the correctness of his build, his proportions, his body angles. Does he have straight legs? Is he free of blemishes, marks? Any sign of strain or injury?

Then I get a feeling for his character. You can tell about his character by the look in a horse's eye and by the way he holds his head. Horses have body language too. How are his stable manners? I look at how he moves, what he looks at. His quickness. Future Vision, for example, a young horse in our stable, has the quickness of a cat. I check his feet, and look at his teeth to determine his age.

I watch him move. Does he move straight? How long a step? Does he push himself forward from the hind end or pull himself forward with the front end? The first few steps he takes out of the stall are important indicators of his soundness. Then I ride him. I find out, and review with him, what he knows. Finally I give him a simple lesson to see how quickly and willingly he learns.

What I look for is a horse that earns eight out of ten on my list of priorities. He has to be sound physically. In his disposition he has to be sufficiently brave and aggressive. You want enough determination and independence, but not so much that you cannot train him. The right balance is critical: too cold, you cannot rev him up; too hot, he boils over all the time.

Critical for show jumping is his ability to shorten and lengthen stride. Course designers are always testing that. The horse must possess those naturally good gaits: walk, trot, and canter. He has to be sufficiently scopey, or powerful, and naturally careful, meaning that, when he sees the jump, he has to naturally want to jump over it without touching it. Some horses do not care if they hit the jump.

The horse must also display basic jumping technique. Some horses have the instinct to jump, others do not. If you throw a ball to a young boy, and he covers his eyes, he obviously does not have the instinct to be

On Big Ben
(Jayne Huddleston)

a good fielder. Another child might instinctively grab it. The first child can perhaps be taught, the second shows a natural ability.

In horses, natural ability is paramount. Humans can compensate for lack of natural ability with motivation, desire, and intelligence. Horses are less able to do that. When I was young, I told myself that by hard work I could compensate for the horse I was about to buy. And in some cases it worked out. But the sport has changed a lot. To win now I have to ride as well as or better than anyone, and have a horse as good as or better than anyone else's. The starting point, then, the horse's natural ability, has become much more important.

Home at Millar Brooke, I contemplate the Royal just past. Three days longer than it used to be, the Royal Winter Fair of 1989 was still the

Mac Cone, Canadian grand prix rider

Unless you can pay your own ticket in our sport, you have to be a good business person. I admire what Ian's doing with syndication, which he pioneered, and in my own way I'm trying to emulate him. So are a lot of other riders.

I remember when we were on the team representing Canada in 1982 at the world championship in Dublin. His main horse at that time — he only had one — was lame. I ended up twenty-second, and you had to make the top twenty to go on to the final day. And Ian, if there were fifty-two in it, he was probably fifty-first. He was at the very bottom of the barrel. Not because of his talent, but because his partners — the good horses — were not there. And I remember standing next to him, and he had that look in his eye. I knew he wasn't going to be in that position very long. That, to me, was the big change in Ian Millar's career. He was at the bottom despite all his talent and ability — but no partners, no horses, no people behind him.

Ian has won two World Cups, and that's a phenomenal thing. But it's not Ian in the ring that's such a cut above the rest. It's his business organization that's so superior to anyone else's in Canada. He beats you with the quality and the numbers of horses in his stable. Before he leaves the farm he's already got the upper hand.

Lynn is a huge, huge part of the whole puzzle. She's just like Ian. She has a good mind. She's educated herself through the years, as he has, to the top level of the sport. She's a shrewd, smart, smart woman. I mean that in a complimentary way. She's tough and strong. I depend on my wife too. It's great to have a partner on the ground. Lynn knows his riding and his horses as well as he does, if not better. I'm in the same situation. My wife knows when I'm on and when I'm off, what I'm doing wrong, and how to fix it.

Everything he does is well thought out. I'm sure if you go into his tack room and look at his bridle rack, you'll see a lot of snaffles [used only on manageable horses], not a lot of warmonger bridles. He selects horses with good minds. He doesn't need a lot of heavy artillery to manage the horse around the course. This all goes back to his being a good horseman. He's shrewd and calculating in his training. He analyses things to the nth degree. He'll end up analysing a horse and a training method like you would construction of the SkyDome or something. He'll carry it that far. That's the way he is. The way he talks and explains everything, he shouldn't be a horseman. He should be prime minister.

national showcase it has long been, but this year the show had trouble attracting the kind of top-flight international competition it has had in the past. European shows have become more attractive, with fatter prizes, and there is consequently less incentive for European riders to go abroad; the Royal, on the other hand, has become too long, with many smaller purses that do not justify a trip overseas. Nevertheless, some fine British, American, and Dutch riders were present, and the wins were still hard to come by.

Pamino did everything we asked of her, winning a first, two seconds, and a fourth in the four classes she contested during the eleven days. Winchester took a second and a fifth, then we sent him home to rest before upcoming events in Europe. The noise and the dust and the crowds had begun to take their toll; he had started to pace in his stall, a measure of his agitation. Big Ben won two seconds and a seventh, and was one of only two horses to go clear in both rounds of the Nations' Cup. One of those seconds was a tie in the grand prix, a World Cup qualifier.

The grand prix was a two-round affair, with survivors of the afternoon round graduating to the evening round on the last Saturday of the Royal. I am sure that the course designer, Linda Allen, would do it differently had she to do it over again. She obviously wanted lots of clear rounds going into the evening, and there were: eleven of them (including Ben and me), plus twelve riders with four faults. Her task in round two was to pare those numbers down — which she did, with giant fences.

I drew the last position, and the grand prix had the makings of a dramatic finish. Only one rider before me, Mac Cone on Pessimist, went without knockdowns in both rounds, but he did pick up a half a fault for time. Mac had to watch from the stands and wonder if that time fault was going to cost him the grand prix. If Big Ben and I went clear within the time allowed, the prize was ours. But my horse became overly enthusiastic galloping the length of the arena to a wide oxer. I knew we were in trouble back at the turn, even before the gallop began. I had too much horse in my hand. Three times I tried to check him, but to no avail. The rail fell, and we had to settle for second — with three others.

I am never glad that a show is over, even one that features only middling success. That is not in my disposition. I enjoy competing too much. Difficult competitions may be the most valuable in the long term for the lessons they offer. Probably mistakes have been made, and they must not be made a second time.

I left the Sixty-first Royal Winter Fair a little run down physically, but happy enough with our results and about $18,000 in prize money. I was the leading international rider, and by the end of the fair I went home knowing that, for the sixth time, I had led the Canadian World Cup Qualifying League in points at the end of the year. In show-jumping terms, the world is divided into seven leagues built around show circuits:

Canada, western Europe, eastern Europe, South America, Mexico, and two leagues in the United States. Certain shows on these circuits are designated World Cup qualifiers. To lead one's league, then, is a notable achievement.

Not bad, I went home thinking, for a rider whose first mounts were dollar-an-hour rental horses named Socks and Flicka.

I mentioned in the Foreword that my first horse, when I was five, was an imaginary horse. A certain amount of fantasy is healthy: it can propel young riders on to greater achievements. However, some forms of fantasy are questionable. I am getting to what is wrong with show jumping in Canada and how, in my view, it has to change.

Riders and horse owners at the grand prix level, for example, may engage in mutual fantasy. The rider, fearful of losing the sponsor's financial backing as well as the horse, perpetuates the myth that over the horizon, or the one after that, lies greatness for this particular horse. Both rider and owner want to believe it, and years can pass before either will face the truth.

Mutual fantasy can also exist at the national level. Miracles do happen, and Canadians, including some riders, begin to believe that Canada is indeed a world power in show jumping. Believers point to important wins in the 1980s: Gail Greenough's world championship, a total of three World Cup victories by Mario Deslauriers and myself, medals at the Pan-American Games and the Rotterdam Alternate Oympics. Canadian horses and riders can and do come up big. We are, after all, dealing with that remarkable animal, the horse. Our sport always holds the possibility of surprise.

But the truth is that our top horses are aging, and the talent coming up through the ranks is thin. Canada has always had a certain number of quality horses and riders, but never in any sort of quantity. For lack of solid horses of international calibre, up to five world-class Canadian riders sit on the sidelines, and that situation has existed for as long as I have been riding.

Meanwhile, the fantasy endures. Competition in Canada, with the exception of Spruce Meadows in Calgary and the Royal Winter Fair in Toronto, tends not to be world-class. The jumps are made lower in the interests of clear rounds and exciting jump-offs. A course designer will keep the vertical jumps at between four feet, nine inches, and five feet, when they should be between five feet and five feet, three inches; or will keep the oxers at five feet wide when they should be six inches to a foot wider. Spectators think the competitions are wonderful, but what they are seeing is often not world-class, and that fact becomes painfully obvious if and when world-class competition comes to town. On paper our Nations' Cup teams look good: lots of grand prix wins on Canadian soil. But as our performances during 1989 in these team events so graphically demonstrate, consistent results often elude us when we are matched against the top European and American teams.

The reason? We lack depth. To win a Nations' Cup, the Canadian team needs four hard-knocking riders, each with two top-of-the-line horses. Anything less and the team is in trouble. In North America there are only four Nations' Cup events the entire year, two in Canada (Calgary and Toronto) and two in the United States (Washington and New York). In Europe there is one nearly every weekend. The British, for example, sometimes use forty different riders throughout the year in these team events. In Canada we might use six or seven.

The solution to beefing up the Canadian equestrian team and the sport in general in this country is threefold. When I sat on a committee established several years ago by Sport Canada to take a hard look at show jumping in this country, we perceived that the big problem was a dearth of quality horses. How do you get more horses? You need more owners. How do you get more owners? You make it more attractive for someone to own a horse.

First, there should be a national circuit of competitions in Canada. "Grand Prix Afternoon in Canada" could be made just as attractive and high-profile as "Hockey Night in Canada". Perhaps the circuit could be held during a season, as with hockey or football, and riders could follow this series of show-jumping events across the country. Shows could work together, enabling riders to move easily from show to show and not have to make choices between shows. A properly timed Canadian circuit would free up Canadian riders to compete both at home and abroad. Promoted, televised, and supported by corporate backing, the national circuit could offer significant prize money and reduced expenses, thus creating real incentives for owners to invest in grand prix horses.

Second — and this follows naturally from the first — those who administer show jumping in Canada have to become more businesslike in their approach. Ratings of televised show-jumping events are consistently high: the sport has some very viable business opportunities now. Convincing corporate interests to sponsor Canadian show-jumping events is not easy, but it is easier than it was. More and more corporate sponsors are realizing that the demographics of the sport are useful or suitable for conveying their corporate messages. In short, the sport appeals to a broad cross-section of society. To capitalize on that, we need a strong, central organization, professionally run and managed. With professionals as the trustees of the sport, and with a continuing and vital role for volunteers, who for decades have run the federal and provincial equestrian federations and all the horse shows, the sport would capitalize on the opportunity that now presents itself.

There has been a certain resistance in our sport to the use of professional managers, but that is changing. More and more Canadian horse shows are professionally run, and why should they not be? Administrators with both the Canadian Equestrian Federation and the Canadian equestrian team have begun to hire professionals — fund-raisers, planners — to make sure the right things happen in the sport. More Canadian riders and trainers, who know how shows *should* be run, are finally getting active in the organization of events.

Third, and finally, there is a role for government to play in the sport of show-jumping, albeit a limited one. Poised for significant growth, show-jumping should be self-sufficient as a spectator sport and as a business worthy of investment. If the federal government were to offer tax incentives, they should be offered to the horse industry as they might be to any industry that generates employment across the country. Studies have shown the tremendous economic impact of horse sports in Canada. Spruce Meadows, for example, exerts a profound economic impact on the city of Calgary by its three annual competitions. That is just one city. Farmers who grow oats and hay, carpenters who build horse barns and arenas, blacksmiths, veterinarians, grooms, sellers of horse products — they all derive work from the industry. The tax structure should not offer tax breaks to people of means who do not need them; surely there are better ways to spend government money. On the other hand, incentives that would encourage participation by investors in the horse industry are entirely appropriate.

On March 10, 1990, my hopes for a third World Cup win aboard Big Ben were dashed. Just weeks before the event was to take place in Dortmund, West Germany, he quite suddenly developed colic that required surgery. Although at the time of writing there is a chance that he will compete in the 1990 World Championships to be held in July in Stockholm, Sweden, I am simply grateful that he is alive and well.

I had ridden him for an hour that morning in Tampa while we were on the Florida circuit. By 2:00 P.M. he was pawing the ground and alternately lying down and standing up — not normal behaviour. Dr. Rick Mitchell, one of the veterinarians at the show, examined him rectally and detected a blockage in the colon. He gave Big Ben medication for pain and we pumped oil into his stomach in an attempt to loosen the blockage.

By that evening the problem had become more acute, and Ben was transferred to the equine hospital in Ocala. Sandi Patterson, who stayed with him throughout the ordeal, Lynn and I, and a great many other people were extremely distressed by the unfolding events. On Sunday morning, after a conference involving Dr. Don Sloane, the attending surgeon, Dr. John Atack, our own vet at Millar Brooke, and myself, we decided to operate. The surgery, a last option, could have meant a year out of Big Ben's career; on the other hand, his life now hung in the balance. Once his digestive system started to shut down, we had no choice.

During surgery, Dr. Sloane found that Big Ben suffered from a twist of the colon. With no need to resection the colon, he simply corrected the twist, and the surgery ended in less than an hour. Several hours for this type of an operation is closer to the norm.

Big Ben, the vets said, then proceeded to make the fastest recovery of any horse they had ever operated on. Strong going into the surgery, Big Ben may surprise us all and compete in Sweden. The horse, like the sport, is full of surprises.

Consider this. You will remember that the feisty Frank Chapot, the American *chef d'équipe*, had deprived Big Ben of an American vet's services during the Pan-American Games in 1987. I felt strongly that prohibiting the vet from treating another team's horse was unsportsman-like. But in 1990, following Big Ben's surgery, I pondered taking another horse to the World Cup Finals, a brand new entry in the Millar Brooke stable called Czar. But the question of our eligibility to compete together at Dortmund was raised in Europe. Certain influential people in North American show jumping took an active role in helping me achieve that eligibility. Who led the fight and was my greatest ally? The same Frank Chapot.

And so I competed with Czar in the 1990 World Cup. But there would be no third consecutive victory for me. John Whitaker on Milton was the winner, though I left West Germany pleased on several counts. We placed twelfth, and Czar was one of only two horses to go clean in the final and toughest phase of this World Cup competition. Lonesome Dove, who had made her European debut only five months beforehand in Stuttgart, placed third in the Grand Prix of Dortmund and won a prestigious class called the Championship of Dortmund, which is held coincidentally with the World Cup.

There will be other World Cup Finals, other competitions, and always new horses — those monarchs among animals that Mrs. Gardiner talked about — to keep me feeling alive and challenged.

Ian Millar's Milestones:

1990 — winner, Canadian Equestrian Federation gold medal for contributions to show jumping in Canada

1989 — first, World Cup Final, Tampa, Florida, on Big Ben
— won ten grand prix victories (a personal best)
— led Canadian World Cup Qualifying League for the sixth time
— ranked first in the world in show-jumping by *l'Année Hippique*

1988 — first, World Cup Final, Göteborg, Sweden, on Big Ben
— ranked third in the world in show-jumping by *l'Année Hippique*
— member of fourth-place team, Olympic Games, Seoul, Korea

1987 — individual and team gold medalist, Pan-American Games, Indianapolis, U.S.A., on Big Ben
— ranked first in the world in show-jumping by *l'Année Hippique*

1986 — awarded the Order of Canada
— first Canadian rider ever to be ranked number one in North America
— second, World Cup Final, Göteborg, Sweden, on Big Ben
— leading international rider at the Royal Winter Fair, Toronto (first Canadian to win the award in more than twenty years)

1984 — member of fourth-place Canadian team, Olympic Games, Los Angeles, U.S.A., on Big Ben

1983 — member of silver-medal-winning Canadian team, Pan-American Games, Caracas, Venezuela, on Foresight

1982 — member of fifth-place Canadian team, world championships, Dublin, Ireland

1980 — member of gold-medal-winning Canadian team at the Alternate Olympic Games, Rotterdam, The Netherlands, on Brother Sam

1979 — individual bronze medalist, Pan-American Games, San Juan, Puerto Rico, on Brother Sam
— member of silver-medal-winning Canadian team, Pan-American Games, San Juan, Puerto Rico, on Brother Sam

1978 — member of fourth-place Canadian team, world championships, Aachen, West Germany, on Brother Sam

1976 — member of fifth-place Canadian team, Olympic Games, Montreal, Quebec, on Countdown

1972 — member of sixth-place Canadian team, Olympic Games, Munich, West Germany, on Shoeman

1971 — named member for the first time of the Canadian equestrian team

ACKNOWLEDGEMENTS

To enter the inward-looking world of show jumping I needed guides — people who speak the arcane language of the sport and of horses — and to them all I owe heartfelt thanks. Especially in the beginning, but right up to deadline, Jayne Huddleston patiently answered hundreds of my questions and painstakingly examined the manuscript at several stages. Maria Meyering of Wilmarny Farm continues the daunting task of teaching me to ride a horse competently. Along with Tiny and Willy Meyering, Maria nurtured my understanding of horses and riders while offering me unbridled encouragement.

Many people too numerous to mention were generous with their time as I struggled to come to grips with the complexities of both Ian Millar and his sport. John Rivington was particularly helpful and open. Eve Mainwaring generously shared her knowledge at Spruce Meadows in Calgary. Randy Roy helped me understand much about my subject. In Stuttgart, Hauke Schmidt and Ulli Kasselmann offered both hospitality and a better understanding of equestrian sport in West Germany. The transcripts of long interviews previously conducted with Ian Millar by Joan Schafer and Peter Thurling in the course of a film project were especially useful. Paula Heinemann, Ian Millar's assistant — and indeed everyone at Millar Brooke farm — was unfailingly kind and keen to advance the book.

Numerous readers, among them David Carpenter, Claudine Carpenter, Glen Allen, Lynne Thomas, Maureen Garvie, Gail Kotchie, Shelley Ambrose, the aforementioned Meyerings, and at least a dozen clients at their riding school, read the manuscript in its various configurations. I valued their insights, criticisms, and support. Jan Whitford, my agent, was professional and personable in equal amounts. The book's editor, Pat Kennedy, made me glad of her editing — no small skill that. Sarah Reid, our copy-editor, used her knowledge of horses to raise some important questions.

Ulrike Bender weathered her husband's brief obsession with the show-jumping world while managing to maintain her own curiosity about the sport. She read and reread the manuscript and remains my first and best editor, and I cannot thank her enough. My three-and-a-half-year-old son, Kurt, who insisted throughout the project that he too was writing a book on Ian Millar, may be finally glad that he has his father back. This book is for friends and family.

Larry Scanlan
Camden East
April 1990